Junior Analytical Grammar: Mechanics

a systematic approach to elementary punctuation, capitalization, and usage

Teacher Book

Created by R. Robin Finley

Junior Analytical Grammar: Mechanics | Teacher Book

Published and distributed by Demme Learning

analyticalgrammar.com

1-888-854-6284 or +1 717-283-1448 | demmelearning.com
Lancaster, Pennsylvania USA

ISBN 978-1-60826-640-1
Revision Code 0110-B

Printed in the United States of America by The P.A. Hutchison Company
2 3 4 5 6 7 8 9 10

For information regarding CPSIA on this printed material call: 1-888-854-6284 and provide reference #0110-07212020

TABLE OF CONTENTS

EDUCATIONAL PHILOSOPHY

I know that home teachers may react to the words "Educational Philosophy" with skepticism since teachers often use it as a screen behind which to hide their own incompetence! There is, however, really no other term to use. I just thought it was important to tell you what my overall vision of the educational process is, and why I think so much of what we call education these days does not, in fact, educate.

I call my educational vision "scaffolding." Visualise a huge office building under construction. It is made up of steel supports and bars which hold all the other stuff on the building together.

Now, imagine an enormous crane with a heavy steel support which is supposed to go on the 9th floor of the building. What would happen if the crane let go of that steel support in midair - in the place where it was supposed to go - BEFORE THE OTHER EIGHT FLOORS HAD BEEN BUILT? The piece of steel would come crashing to the ground!

If, however, the first eight floors have been well-built beforehand, then that piece of steel would rest snugly and permanently in its proper place.

The reason that so much of what we teach (especially in the language arts area - notably in punctuation) isn't retained is because we haven't carefully built the basic structure of knowledge necessary for that retention. So the new knowledge doesn't "stick"!

A fair number of punctuation rules are based on the knowledge of advanced grammar, and so we have not included these in this book. We have instead chosen to use the punctuation marks that we believe your student(s) can retain based on the grammar they have been able to master by doing either Junior Analytical Grammar or the first "season" of Analytical Grammar.

It is very important that you understand that Junior Analytical Grammar Mechanics **should not be attempted unless and until your student has completed either Junior Analytical Grammar or the first "season" of Analytical Grammar.** In other words, these are pre-requisites for this book. If you attempt to teach these punctuation, capitalization, and usage rules without your student having completed the pre-requisites, you are setting him or her - and yourself! - up for a great deal of frustration.

If your student has not completed either Jr. Analytical Grammar or the first "season" of AG, he or she should have done enough formal grammar to be able to easily dissect simple and compound sentences by labeling (parsing) AND diagraming them.

You will notice that we don't address issues of "end punctuation" and the capitalization of the first word of a sentence. Since Junior Analytical Grammar is not recommended until 4th or 5th grade, we assume you will have already addressed these skills in your early elementary curriculum.

NOTES FOR HOMETEACHERS

As a general rule, I recommend that you take at least one week for each unit in this course. I will map out what you can do day-by-day.

DAY #1: First **"Talk through" the notes with your student.**

Side note: When asking a student for a correct answer, teachers often don't give them time to think because they are afraid that perhaps the child doesn't know the answer. So they either rephrase the question to make it easier or they answer the question for him. I believe that this teaches the student two things: #1) "The teacher doesn't think I can answer this." and #2) "If I don't answer right away, I'm off the hook!" It is also not uncommon for students to pretend they don't know an answer as a way of "passive resistance."

In my classroom, I have been known to ask a question of a student (who I know can answer the question, but is resisting me) and wait for a LONG time for an answer. Eventually (just to make me go away!) the student answers the question. Then I've got him! Because once you know you can do something successfully, you want to keep on doing it!

So give your students time by waiting quietly. Rephrase or prompt only if you're <u>sure</u> he or she doesn't know. Keep on until you have "talked through" the notes.

Then, work with your student on the first one or two sentences in Exercise #1. Then ask the student to complete the exercise. Emphasize that <u>by all means</u> the students should consult the notes for help in doing the exercise.

Day #2: Using the answer key for Exercise #1, go over the answers with your student. You are particularly interested in any mistakes your student has made. There are two kinds of mistakes: the first is a mistake which, once the student sees the right answer, he understands why he got it wrong. The second is the most important kind. That's a mistake which the student has made and he doesn't know why. These mistakes mean that you and the student need to go back to the notes and review.

Once Exercise #1 has been reviewed for accuracy, give the student Exercise #2. Again, emphasize that he should use the notes for help.

Day #3: Review the answers on Exercise #2 in the same manner as you did Exercise #1. Give the student Exercise #3. Remind him to use his notes if necessary.

Day #4: Review the answers on Exercise #3 as you did with Exercises #1 and #2.

Day #5: The test can be given to the student on Day #4, or you may want to wait a day and give the assessment on Day #5. I don't think either way is better than the other. Your student will probably let you know which works best for him.

I think it's a good idea to correct the test with the student so mistakes are immediately apparent. If a student answers at least 70% in each section of the assessment (that's the Competency level) correctly, he or she should move on. When the test has been corrected, you can go to the next unit and start the process all over again.

Correcting tests containing punctuation is a bit different from correcting grammar tests. That's because it's just as important to know when a comma is *not* supposed to be there as it is to know when it's supposed to be there. So the rule of thumb should be that BAD PUNCTUATION CANCELS OUT GOOD PUNCTUATION. It would be a good idea to emphasize to your student that he/she should not put in any punctuation unless he/she knows the rule being applied. In other words, don't put in punctuation because, "I don't know; it just looks right"! If a sentence is supposed to have one comma in it - and it's worth one point - and your student puts that comma in plus another one, he will earn the point for the correct comma and lose it again for the incorrect comma.

Also if you look at the Unit #2 test, sentence #1, you'll notice that it's worth two points, even though there's only one comma on the test key. That's because there should NOT be a comma between *shiny* and *red*. (If you apply the "and" test, you realize that you'd never say "shiny and red car." So you don't want to put a comma there.)

THE "CHEAT SHEET"

Before you start this book, get yourself a nice big piece of posterboard or construction paper and put it up somewhere where your student can easily see it. As you go through each punctuation, capitalization, or usage rule, you will be given a "buzzword." That's a short, descriptive title for that rule. Write that "buzzword" up on your "cheat sheet" so that your student can easily refer to it as he or she does the exercises and takes the tests. Underneath each "buzzword," write an example sentence to show how it works. I think both you and your student will find that the "cheat sheet" will take the pressure off and help him or her remember the rules you're teaching.

We also highly recommend that you put the copy editing symbols on your "cheat sheet." All the copy editing symbols are listed in the unit where that rule is introduced.

When you're finished with JAG: Mechanics, work on incorporating and holding your child accountable for all these rules in his or her writing assignments. Your next step is to start Analytical Grammar when you feel your child is ready. AG can be used as early as 6th grade, and there are a number of flexible scheduling options for it. Also consider using Beyond the Book Report along with Analytical Grammar. It's our literature study and writing program specifically designed to be used and scheduled with AG.

COMMA SPLITS

You're about to learn about commas. A comma is a little piece of punctuation that tells us to pause when we read or speak or divide a sentence into more understandable parts. We really need commas! Take a look at this example:

I like peanut butter and jelly and mom and dad enjoy bacon lettuce and tomato.

Did it take you a try or two to figure out that sentence? Now try it with commas:

I like peanut butter and jelly, and mom and dad enjoy bacon, lettuce, and tomato.

Ahhh ... it's SO much easier to read!

There are rules that tell us where commas should go. There are also rules about where commas should not go! We'll start there first.

A COMMA SPLIT is when you put a comma where it doesn't belong. ***Here is a list of places where a comma should not be*****:**

1. There should never be ONE comma between a SUBJECT and a VERB.

   EXAMPLE: The dog, walked into the garage.

2. There should never be ONE comma between a VERB and ITS DIRECT OBJECT.

   EXAMPLE: The man threw, the ball.

3. There should never be ONE comma between a LINKING VERB and ITS COMPLEMENT. (a complement is a predicate adjective or a predicate nominative)

   EXAMPLE: The girl felt, wonderful! *or* That girl is, my sister.

4. There should never be ONE comma between a MODIFIER and ITS NOUN. *(the modifier right before the noun)*

   EXAMPLE: The soft, blue, fluffy, sweater was beautiful.

5. There should never be ONE comma between a VERB and ITS INDIRECT OBJECT.

   EXAMPLE: I wrote, my aunt a letter.

6. There shouldn't be ONE comma between an INDIRECT OBJECT and ITS DIRECT OBJECT.

   EXAMPLE: I wrote my aunt, a letter.

(over)

In the comma rule exercises and tests, you'll need to refer to these comma split notes to help answer the questions. You'll start learning the comma rules right away, but it's also important for you to really understand the comma splits as well!

REMEMBER THE SIX DEADLY SPLITS!

1. Subject and verb

2. Verb and direct object

3. Linking verb and complement

4. Modifier and its noun

5. Verb and indirect object

6. Indirect object and direct object

Throughout this book you will have exercises in copy-editing. When you copy-edit, you correct mistakes you see in sentences. Sometimes you will add something where it is missing, remove something that should not be there, or change something that is incorrect.

There are certain symbols we use to copy-edit. As we move through this book, you will be taught the symbols you need to know.

Here are your first two symbols:

To add a comma - red white, and blue

To remove a comma (or anything else in the future) - remove ~~this~~

COMMAS: ITEMS IN A SERIES

Each of our comma rules will have a "buzzword" that we'll use to refer to it. Our first rule is "items in a series."

ITEMS IN A SERIES: Use commas in between items in a list or series. These can be individual words or prepositional phrases, but the list should always be made of grammatical equals (all nouns, all verbs, all prepositional phrases, etc.) You will put a comma between each item and before the conjuction that will come before the last item.

EXAMPLES *(these are only a few examples, there are a lot of other ways to list things)*:

Nouns - I brought my ball, bat, mitt, and hat to the baseball game.

Verbs - I walked, ran, hopped, and jumped to get my exercise in today.

Adjectives - She was tall, slim, and beautiful.

Prepositional phrases - We looked in the kitchen, around the dining room table, and on top of the fridge for the artwork my sister made.

Nouns and prepositional phrases - My chore list says to put the dishes in the dish-washer, the glasses in the cabinet, and the trash in the trashcan.

Verbs and prepositional phrases - Little red riding hood walked through the woods, skipped down the lane, and entered her grandmother's house.

NOTE: If all the items are separated by "and" or "or," do not use commas to separate them.

EXAMPLE: I bought a teddy bear and a necklace and a new shirt.

(over)

NOTE #2: The comma before the last item (usually before the conjunction) is sometimes called the auxiliary or Oxford comma. Some people are taught that it can be left out. Not us! You can confuse people by leaving it out, so we always include it.

EXAMPLE: On my desk I have pictures of my parents, Spot and Whiskers.

Are you giggling? I would be! It makes it seem that Spot and Whiskers are the speaker's parents. Now put the auxiliary comma in.

EXAMPLE: On my desk I have pictures of my parents, Spot, and Whiskers.

NOW I get it! Those are three separate pictures!

HERE'S A TRICK: If you read the sentences above out loud, just the way you'd say them in real life, your voice will pause right where the commas go. So if you have to put commas in a sentence where we've left the commas out on purpose, read the sentence out loud first, and your voice will tell you where they go!

The buzzword for this rule is *"items in a series."*

ITEMS IN A SERIES: EXERCISE #1

NAME: ____

WHAT TO DO: In each sentence, insert the commas where they should go.

1. My brother, mother, sister, and I went on a trip to the mall.

2. We had to find shoes for my brother, a hat for my sister, and a new skirt for me.

3. My brother found some tennis shoes that were red, white, and black.

4. I yelled, screamed, and waved my arms to get mom's attention.

5. Mom had to walk through the racks, around a display, and over to the corner to find me.

6. I found the perfect skirt made of denim, cotton, and eyelet.

WHAT TO DO: Copy-edit the errors in the following sentences. There are five errors.

I asked, mom if she would buy me the skirt I needed. I needed wanted and desired that skirt! Mom looked at the beautiful, skirt on the hanger and told me to try it on. I went in the dressing room, closed the door and tried on the skirt.

ITEMS IN A SERIES: EXERCISE #2

NAME: ______________________________

WHAT TO DO: In each sentence, insert the commas where they should go.

1. The skirt was twirly, swirly, and girly!

2. Mom said we could buy the skirt, leave the store, and look for a hat for my sister.

3. We went to the check out counter, paid for the skirt, and got our change.

4. We looked, searched, and finally discovered a hat store.

5. My sister needed a hat that she could wear at the beach, the pool, and the backyard.

WHAT TO DO: Copy-edit the errors in the following sentences. There are five errors.

It's always, a good idea to wear a hat when you're out in the sun. The hat can be made of straw, or cotton, or polyester! What is important is that it protects you from the sun's UVA rays, UVB rays, and heat. Protect, your face from the sun!

ITEMS IN A SERIES: EXERCISE #3

NAME: ____

WHAT TO DO: In each sentence, insert the commas where they should go.

1. My sister walked into the store, up through the aisle, and up to the counter.

2. She asked the clerk which hat would be best for the beach, the backyard, and the pool.

3. The clerk was helpful, cheerful, and knowledgeable.

4. We watched the clerk circle the store, select hats, and help my sister.

5. My sister was happy with her new hat for the beach, pool, and backyard.

WHAT TO DO: Copy-edit the errors in the following sentences. There are five errors.

By this time mom was tired of walking around the mall spending money. My sister brother and I told her how much we appreciated the shopping trip. Mom smiled and said she was happy to take us. We kids were proud that we were well-behaved, appreciative and fun.

TEST: ITEMS IN A SERIES

NAME: ______________________________

POINTS EARNED: ________ out of 15 ____ LEVEL: ________________

WHAT TO DO: In each sentence, insert the commas where they should go.

__/2 1. It was time to head to the food court and eat, eat, and eat!

__/2 2. Mom and my sister wanted pizza, my brother wanted chicken, and I wanted a salad.

__/2 3. The pizza was covered in pepperoni, mushrooms, and olives.

__/2 4. My brother's system for dipping chicken was to use ketchup, barbeque sauce, and honey mustard.

__/2 5. My salad was artfully created with celery on the left, tomatoes on the right, and cheese in the middle.

WHAT TO DO: Copy-edit the errors in the following sentences. There are five errors.

__/5 After we ate it was, time to head home. We pulled dragged, and pushed our packages to the car. Thank goodness there, was room in the trunk for it all! My mom, sister brother, and I talked all the way home. We had, a great time going to the mall as a family.

===
15

(over)

Points Range		Level
15 - 14	=	Mastery
13 - 12	=	Superiority
11 - 10	=	Competency
9 - 8	=	Probationary
7 and below	=	Repeat

COMMAS: TWO ADJECTIVES "AND TEST"

The buzzword for this rule is *"two adjectives 'and test.'"*

TWO ADJECTIVES "AND TEST": You will SOMETIMES use a comma in between two or more adjectives that come before a noun. It's that "sometimes" that makes you nervous, right? How are you supposed to know when you need a comma between two adjectives and when you don't? That's where the "and test" comes in!

The "and test" works like this: If it sounds very natural to put the word "and" in between the adjectives, you need a comma. If "and" sounds funny at all, forget the comma.

EXAMPLE #1:

That is a lovely soft fuzzy sweater.

(... a lovely AND soft sweater? ... sounds good - you need a comma)

(... a soft AND fuzzy sweater? ... sounds good - you need a comma)

It should be: That is a lovely, soft, fuzzy sweater.

EXAMPLE #2:

I saw a little old man.

(... a little AND old man? ... sounds weird- forget the comma)

It should be: I saw a little old man.

TWO ADJECTIVES "AND TEST": EXERCISE #1

NAME: ______________________________

WHAT TO DO: In each sentence, insert the commas where they should go. If the sentence is correct as written, just leave it blank.

1. My friends and I went to the enormous, exciting playground near the library.

2. Sarah is my friend with the long black hair.

3. Johnny has freckles and his hair is the color of a ripe, tasty carrot.

4. Naomi likes to wear denim overalls with bright, colorful patches on the knees.

5. I have the most wonderful, lively group of friends in the world.

WHAT TO DO: Copy-edit the errors in the following sentences. There are five errors.

A good, old group of buddies is a wonderful thing. We like to hang out and, play with each other. We sometimes fight about, silly things. I suppose that happens in all groups of close, friends. We always make up and give each other a sincere heart-felt apology.

(over)

WHAT TO DO: In each sentence below there is a comma split. In the spaces below each sentence are the numbers of all the commas in the sentence. Find the comma split and write its number in the space at the left. Write what it is splitting beside that comma's number below the sentence. Next to the other numbers, write the buzzword of the comma rule for that comma.

Example:

1 We find, many fun, exciting things to do at the playground.
1 2

#1 *splits verb and direct object*

#2 *two adjectives "and test"*

---

1 1. To get to the library, playground I go up the street,
1 2

around the corner, and to the right.
3

#1 *splits noun and its modifier*

#2 *items in a series*

#3 *items in a series*

2 2. My wonderful, amazing dad, dropped me off there.
1 2

#1 *two adjectives "and test"*

#2 *splits subject and verb*

TWO ADJECTIVES "AND TEST": EXERCISE #2

NAME: ____

WHAT TO DO: In each sentence, insert the commas where they should go. If the sentence is correct as written, just leave it blank.

1. My friends and I had to decide what thrilling, enjoyable thing to do first!

2. Bouncy, joyful Sarah decided to start on the trampoline.

3. Calm, cool, collected Johnny chose the swings.

4. Crazy, thrill-seeking Naomi wanted to try the super slide!

5. I wanted to do my loud, obnoxious monkey impression on the monkey bars.

WHAT TO DO: Copy-edit the errors in the following sentences. There are five errors.

We all decided it would be, fun to see who could do the most outrageous, hilarious tricks. Sarah did flips, jumps, and kicks on the trampoline. I hung from the monkey, bars with only one leg. Johnny, won by doing a huge flip off the end of the swing!

(over)

WHAT TO DO: In each sentence below there is a comma split. In the spaces below each sentence are the numbers of all the commas in the sentence. Find the comma split and write its number in the space at the left. Write what it is splitting beside that comma's number below the sentence. Next to the other numbers, write the buzzword of the comma rule for that comma.

1 1. We were, mad at Johnny for his dangerous, crazy stunt.
1 2

#1 *splits linking verb and complement*

#2 *two adjectives "and test"*

1 2. He, could have hurt his arm, leg, or head doing that trick!
1 2 3

#1 *splits subject and verb*

#2 *items in a series*

#3 *items in a series*

2 3. Next time wild, foolish Johnny should do, a trick that is hilarious and safe.
1 2

#1 *two adjectives "and test"*

#2 *splits verb and direct object*

TWO ADJECTIVES "AND TEST": EXERCISE #3

NAME: ____________________

WHAT TO DO: In each sentence, insert the commas where they should go. If the sentence is correct as written, just leave it blank.

1. All of a sudden we felt a cool, blustery wind.

2. You could see the grey billowy clouds coming toward us.

3. It had been such a bright, shiny morning!

4. Could it really be a wet, sloppy, soaking rainstorm coming?

5. Then we jumped like frightened, trembling mice when we heard the thunder give a tremendous booming crack!

WHAT TO DO: Copy-edit the errors in the following sentences. There are five errors.

Not one of us had, thought to bring an umbrella. We searched around the playground for a table, slide or board we could huddle under. There was one little, old picnic table off to the side. We crouched under those splintered stained, pieces of wood to keep dry.

(over)

WHAT TO DO: In each sentence below there is a comma split. In the spaces below each sentence are the numbers of all the commas in the sentence. Find the comma split and write its number in the space at the left. Write what it is splitting beside that comma's number below the sentence. Next to the other numbers, write the buzzword of the comma rule for that comma.

1 1. Dad must have seen, the windy, wet rainstorm coming.
(comma numbers: 1, 2)

#1 *splits verb and direct object*

#2 *two adjectives "and test"*

1 2. We, saw my dad's car come around the corner, up the driveway, and into the parking lot.
(comma numbers: 1, 2, 3)

#1 *splits subject and verb*

#2 *items in a series*

#3 *items in a series*

2 3. Four soaked, shivering kids climbed into dad's, car.
(comma numbers: 1, 2)

#1 *two adjectives "and test"*

#2 *splits noun and its modifier*

TEST: TWO ADJECTIVES "AND TEST"

NAME: ______________________________

POINTS EARNED: ________ out of 26 ____ LEVEL: ______________

WHAT TO DO: In each sentence, insert the commas where they should go. If the sentence is correct as written, just leave it blank.

__ 1. Dad's huge, shiny red car drove us to my house.
2

__ 2. The rag-tag, dripping kids ran up to the front door.
1

__ 3. We were excited to see four cups of steaming hot chocolate!
1

__ 4. We had towels around our shivering wet shoulders.
1

__ 5. My friends and I gathered around the table in my warm, comfortable kitchen.
1

WHAT TO DO: Copy-edit the errors in the following sentences. There are five errors.

Sarah got us all laughing, giggling, and snorting when she told us we looked like drowned, rats. We had warmed up and were now telling funny, knee-slapping jokes to each other. Mom gave, us each a chewy, gooey chocolate brownie to go with our hot chocolate.

__
5

===
11

(over)

WHAT TO DO: In each sentence below there is a comma split. In the spaces below each sentence are the numbers of all the commas in the sentence. Find the comma split and write its number in the space at the left. Write what it is splitting beside that comma's number below the sentence. Next to the other numbers, write the buzzword of the comma rule for that comma.

3 (2)

1. Now our tummies were filled, (1) our clothes were dry, (2) and our bodies were, (3) warmed.

(1) #1 *items in a series*

(1) #2 *items in a series*

(1) #3 *splits linking verb and complement*

(5)

1 (2)

2. We, (1) had a comical, (2) strange, (3) crazy day!

(1) #1 *splits subject and verb*

(1) #2 *two adjectives "and test"*

(1) #3 *two adjectives "and test"*

(5)

1 (2)

3. I am, (1) lucky to have friends like Sarah, (2) Johnny, (3) and Naomi.

(1) #1 *splits linking verb and complement*

(1) #2 *items in a series*

(1) #3 *items in a series*

(5)

Points Range		**Level**
26 - 23	=	Mastery
22 - 21	=	Superiority
20 - 18	=	Competency
17 - 16	=	Probationary
15 and below	=	Repeat

15

COMMAS: COMPOUND SENTENCE

The buzzword for this rule is *"compound sentence."*

Sometimes we will say or write two sentences together like this:

I cleaned up my room. My sister washed the dishes.

That's fine. There's nothing wrong with that. But sometimes it just seems like those sentences need to be connected more. They relate to each other. That's when you can do this:

I cleaned up my room, and my sister washed the dishes.

Do you see how the meaning is a little different that way? By combining the sentences, you can show a relationship between the two.

COMPOUND SENTENCE: Use a comma before the conjunction when it joins independent clauses (or sentences).

Be careful that you really have two complete sentences, though. Look at this example:

I cleaned up my room and washed the dishes.

There should be no comma in this sentence because what comes after the conjunction is not a complete sentence.

Now may be a good time to review the Unit #11 notes in your *Junior Analytical Grammar* book. The example above is very similar to part B, example #2 of those notes (compound verb).

Now look at example H on those notes (compound sentence). This is a great example of the following exception.

(over)

EXCEPTION TO THE COMPOUND SENTENCE RULE:

IF you are using the conjunction "and,"

and

IF either of the sentences contains four words or less,

DO NOT USE A COMMA.

Example: I cleaned up my room and my sister vacuumed.
(no commas because the second sentence is only three words long.)

But remember that this exception only applies when the conjunction is **AND.** If you used the same sentence above and substituted the conjunction *but*, or any other conjunction such as *or*, *nor*, or *yet*, you'd need a comma.

COMPOUND SENTENCE: EXERCISE #1

NAME: ____

WHAT TO DO: In each sentence, insert the commas where they should go. If the sentence is correct as written, just leave it blank.

1. Our bodies are amazing things, and we should keep them healthy.

2. Every day I try to get some exercise, but sometimes my schedule gets too busy.

3. I enjoy playing basketball and biking with my friends.

4. There are many ways to exercise, and running is one of them.

5. A good game of tag is great exercise and it's fun too!

WHAT TO DO: Copy-edit the errors in the following sentences. There are five errors.

I always make sure to carry cold, ice water with me when I exercise. It's important to keep, your body hydrated. I feel nauseous, dizzy and ill when I get dehydrated. I don't like that feeling and I do what I can to make sure that doesn't happen. Hydrating, is the best way to feel great while you play!

(over)

WHAT TO DO: In each sentence below there is a comma split. In the spaces below each sentence are the numbers of all the commas in the sentence. Find the comma split and write its number in the space at the left. Write what it is splitting beside that comma's number below the sentence. Next to the other numbers, write the buzzword of the comma rule for that comma.

1 1. I, enjoy aerobic, strengthening, and stretching execises.
1 2 3

#1 *splits subject and verb*

#2 *items in a series*

#3 *items in a series*

2 2. I stretch for ten minutes, and I lift, weights for 20 minutes.
1 2

#1 *compound sentence*

#2 *splits verb and direct object*

1 3. A favorite, exercise of mine is fast, energetic dancing!
1 2

#1 *splits noun and its modifier*

#2 *two adjectives "and test"*

COMPOUND SENTENCE: EXERCISE #2

NAME: ______________________________

WHAT TO DO: In each sentence, insert the commas where they should go. If the sentence is correct as written, just leave it blank.

1. My parents and I went to the lake this morning, and we went for a long walk.

2. I make sure to wear proper walking shoes and bring my water bottle.

3. The trail around the lake is nice, and the fresh air felt great!

4. Mom walks fast, but I walk faster.

5. I brought our dog, and we all enjoyed the exercise.

WHAT TO DO: Copy-edit the errors in the following sentences. There are five errors.

Dogs, need exercise! Sparky loves to play fetch, chase his tail and go for long walks. All these things are great, exercise for him. Sparky is a healthy happy dog. I love my dog, and my dog loves me!

(over)

WHAT TO DO: In each sentence below there is a comma split. In the spaces below each sentence are the numbers of all the commas in the sentence. Find the comma split and write its number in the space at the left. Write what it is splitting beside that comma's number below the sentence. Next to the other numbers, write the buzzword of the comma rule for that comma.

1 1. We always, feed the ducks at the end of our long, lovely walk.
(comma 1 after "always"; comma 2 after "long")

#1 *splits subject and verb*

#2 *two adjectives "and test"*

1 2. Mom brings, some tasty saltines, and I bring the soft bread.
(comma 1 after "brings"; comma 2 after "saltines")

#1 *splits verb and direct object*

#2 *compound sentence*

3 3. The ducks quack, the gulls dive, and the geese, squawk!
(comma 1 after "quack"; comma 2 after "dive"; comma 3 after "geese")

#1 *items in a series*

#2 *items in a series*

#3 *splits subject and verb*

COMPOUND SENTENCE: EXERCISE #3

NAME: ______________________________

WHAT TO DO: In each sentence, insert the commas where they should go. If the sentence is correct as written, just leave it blank.

1. My dad's favorite exercise is playing basketball, and I love playing soccer.

2. My sister likes hockey, but she doesn't get to play very often.

3. My brother is the quarterback for our football team, and he practices all the time.

4. Mom plays tennis and she competes in tournaments.

5. We all try to keep active and try to stay healthy.

WHAT TO DO: Copy-edit the errors in the following sentences. There are five errors.

It is always, important to be safe when you exercise. For some sports you'll need protection for your eyes, head, and body. Many people wear safety, glasses. Football and hockey players wear pads, and helmets. The helmets protect them from getting a horrible, painful head injury.

(over)

WHAT TO DO: In each sentence below there is a comma split. In the spaces below each sentence are the numbers of all the commas in the sentence. Find the comma split and write its number in the space at the left. Write what it is splitting beside that comma's number below the sentence. Next to the other numbers, write the buzzword of the comma rule for that comma.

__**1**__ 1. Some, sports are played by teams, and some are played by individuals.
(comma numbers: Some, = 1; teams, = 2)

#1 *splits noun and its modifier*

#2 *compound sentence*

__**1**__ 2. Team sports and individual sports, are great ways to break a strong, healthy sweat!
(comma numbers: sports, = 1; strong, = 2)

#1 *splits subject and verb*

#2 *two adjectives "and test"*

__**2**__ 3. Playing sports is really entertaining, and the exercise is, good for you!
(comma numbers: entertaining, = 1; is, = 2)

#1 *compound sentence*

#2 *splits linking verb and complement*

TEST: COMPOUND SENTENCE

NAME: ______________________________

POINTS EARNED:__________ out of 24____ LEVEL: ________________

WHAT TO DO: In each sentence, insert the commas where they should go. If the sentence is correct as written, just leave it blank.

__1. There are a lot of ways to get exercise, but you have to make the effort.
1

__2. Don't take the elevator to go up and walk where you can.
1

__3. Ask your parents to park far away from your destination, and the walk will do you good!
1

__4. I've heard it said that each stair you take adds time to your life, and I think it is true.
1

__5. Walking up stairs takes more time but gives you better health.
1

WHAT TO DO: Copy-edit the errors in the following sentences. There are five errors.

The worst part, about exercising is the stinky, sweaty clothes! Mom always yells at me if mine end up on the floor, the bed, or the countertop. I suppose that's what the hamper is for, and I, need to put them in there!

__
5

===
10

(over)

WHAT TO DO: In each sentence below there is a comma split. In the spaces below each sentence are the numbers of all the commas in the sentence. Find the comma split and write its number in the space at the left. Write what it is splitting beside that comma's number below the sentence. Next to the other numbers, write the buzzword of the comma rule for that comma.

1 (__/2)

1. Put down the video game,(1) controller,(2) put on your shoes,(3) and go outside and play tag!

__/1 #1 *splits noun and its modifier*

__/1 #2 *items in a series*

__/1 #3 *items in a series*

1 (__/2)

2. I,(1) enjoy watching TV,(2) but that's no way to get a strong,(3) healthy body.

__/1 #1 *splits subject and verb*

__/1 #2 *compound sentence*

__/1 #3 *two adjectives "and test"*

1 (__/2)

3. I get,(1) my heart rate up every day,(2) and you should do the same thing!

__/1 #1 *splits verb and direct object*

__/1 #2 *compound sentence*

Points Range		Level
24 - 22	=	Mastery
21 - 19	=	Superiority
18 - 17	=	Competency
16 - 14	=	Probationary
13 and below	=	Repeat

===
14

COMMAS: INTRODUCTORY ELEMENTS

We will learn two different comma rules in this unit. Are you ready? You can do it!

I. Introductory Single Word

The buzzword for this rule is *"introductory single word."*

There are many times when a word comes at the beginning of a sentence, but serves no real purpose. These are words such as *yes*, *well*, *no*, *why*, *say,* and *oh*. Whenever this happens, all you need to do is put a comma after that word. If you read it out loud, you'll usually pause.

Examples:

Oh, that's not the right answer!
Why, of course I'll come to dinner!
Yes, that's my favorite book.

II. Two or more introductory prepositional phrases

The buzzword for this rule is *"two or more introductory prepositional phrases."*
(Yup, it's a long buzzword! You can shorten it to *"2+ intro prep phrases."*)

Whenever you have AT LEAST TWO prepositional phrases at the beginning of a sentence, you'll need to put a comma after the last one.

Examples:
In the corner on the table, you'll find that letter.
Near the door in the stand with the umbrellas, you'll find your cane.

NOTE: If there is only one prepositional phrase at the beginning of the sentence, no comma is necessary **UNLESS the sentence would be confusing without it.** Look at the sentence below and try to imagine it without the comma. Why would it be confusing?

In the mail, boxes arrived from my grandmother.

If the comma weren't there, you - at first - would think that we were talking about "mail boxes," right? If the last word of the prepositional phrase looks like it could modify the next word in the sentence, use a comma. *(over)*

INTRODUCTORY ELEMENTS: EXERCISE #1

NAME: ____

WHAT TO DO: In each sentence, insert the commas where they should go. If the sentence is correct as written, just leave it blank.

1. In a corner of my room, there is my little bird's cage.

2. By the light of the morning sun, she chirps her good morning.

3. Why, it's a great way to wake up to a new day!

4. Yes, my little songbird is a good friend.

5. In a little while she'll sing again.

WHAT TO DO: Copy-edit the errors in the following sentences. There are five errors.

My little bird's name, is Belle. She's a lovely soft shade of yellow. On my last birthday in March I asked for a pet. I knew a bird would be a great friend and my mom and dad said I could have one. I told mom and dad I would feed her, clean her cage and groom her feathers.

WHAT TO DO: In each sentence below there is a comma split. In the spaces below each sentence are the numbers of all the commas in the sentence. Find the comma split and write its number in the space at the left. Write what it is splitting beside that comma's number below the sentence. Next to the other numbers, write the buzzword of the comma rule for that comma.

1 1. My, family has always had a cat, a dog, or a bird.
(comma numbers: 1 after "My," 2 after "cat," 3 after "dog,")

#1 *splits noun and its modifier*

#2 *items in a series*

#3 *items in a series*

2 2. On the couch in our living room, you, will find our fat, lazy cat.
(comma numbers: 1 after "room," 2 after "you," 3 after "fat,")

#1 *two+ intro prep phrases*

#2 *splits subject and verb*

#3 *two adjectives "and test"*

3 3. Yes, Heathcliff is fat, but we love, him.
(comma numbers: 1 after "Yes," 2 after "fat," 3 after "love,")

#1 *introductory single word*

#2 *compound sentence*

#3 *splits verb and direct object*

INTRODUCTORY ELEMENTS: EXERCISE #2

NAME: ____

WHAT TO DO: In each sentence, insert the commas where they should go. If the sentence is correct as written, just leave it blank.

1. Why, I had no idea you could have a snake for a pet!

2. On a table in my friend's room, you'll see her snake.

3. Yes, his name really is Snuggles.

4. In the wild, snakes can attack.

5. No, Snuggles would never do that!

WHAT TO DO: Copy-edit the errors in the following sentences. There are five errors.

Some people have ferrets, pigs, or lizards as pets. An animal, may seem a strange pet to you, but another person may love that animal as a pet. Giving a pet a loving, caring home is very important. In the end, that is all that matters.

(over)

WHAT TO DO: In each sentence below there is a comma split. In the spaces below each sentence are the numbers of all the commas in the sentence. Find the comma split and write its number in the space at the left. Write what it is splitting beside that comma's number below the sentence. Next to the other numbers, write the buzzword of the comma rule for that comma.

__**1**__ 1. Snuggles got out of his, cage one afternoon, and he went on a mission to explore my friend's huge, two-story house.
(commas numbered 1, 2, 3)

#1 *splits noun and its modifier*

#2 *compound sentence*

#3 *two adjectives "and test"*

__**2**__ 2. Well, we found, him curled up in her dad's comfy chair!
(commas numbered 1, 2)

#1 *introductory single word*

#2 *splits verb and direct object*

__**1**__ 3. At least he, wasn't eating Cheetos, watching a movie, and drinking a root beer!
(commas numbered 1, 2, 3)

#1 *splits subject and verb*

#2 *items in a series*

#3 *items in a series*

INTRODUCTORY ELEMENTS: EXERCISE #3

NAME: ____

WHAT TO DO: In each sentence, insert the commas where they should go. If the sentence is correct as written, just leave it blank.

1. For my birthday in January, my parents gave me a dog.

2. Yes, I had been dreaming and hoping for a dog for years!

3. During my search for the perfect dog, I discovered greyhounds.

4. Beyond their lives as racing dogs, greyhounds make great pets.

5. Oh, I was so excited to finally have a greyhound of my own!

WHAT TO DO: Copy-edit the errors in the following sentences. There are five errors.

Greyhounds have long sleek bodies, and they are designed to race. Yes these dogs are fast, but they are, gentle. Greyhounds are bred to race, and are usually adopted as adult dogs when they retire. These dogs are so happy to be loved, cared for and protected.

(over)

WHAT TO DO: In each sentence below there is a comma split. In the spaces below each sentence are the numbers of all the commas in the sentence. Find the comma split and write its number in the space at the left. Write what it is splitting beside that comma's number below the sentence. Next to the other numbers, write the buzzword of the comma rule for that comma.

2 1. In the morning after breakfast, my friend and I will take our dogs to the dog, park.

(commas numbered: breakfast, = 1; dog, = 2)

#1 *two+ intro prep phrases*

#2 *splits noun and its modifier*

2 2. It's great to see the dogs exercise and play, and we, love spending quality time with them.

(commas numbered: play, = 1; we, = 2)

#1 *compound sentence*

#2 *splits subject and verb*

1 3. Our, dogs run, play fetch, and chase each other all morning at the dog park!

(commas numbered: Our, = 1; run, = 2; fetch, = 3)

#1 *splits noun and its modifier*

#2 *items in a series*

#3 *items in a series*

TEST: INTRODUCTORY ELEMENTS

NAME: ______________________________

POINTS EARNED: __________ out of 25 ____ LEVEL: ______________

WHAT TO DO: In each sentence, insert the commas where they should go. If the sentence is correct as written, just leave it blank.

__ 1. On the corner of Main Street, there is a little pet shop.
1

__ 2. Yes, I decided to get a new pet!
1

__ 3. For my new pet I decided to get a gerbil.
1

__ 4. Oh, they are so soft and cute!
1

__ 5. On the shelf in my room, I have a new cage all ready.
1

WHAT TO DO: Copy-edit the errors in the following sentences. There are five errors.

My trip to the pet shop was a lot of fun, but it made me feel a little sad too. In the cages/ there were puppies, kittens, and mice. Oh, I wanted to take them all home with me! I wish all animals could find good homes, and I'm going to make sure my pets are well taken care of.

__
5

===
10

WHAT TO DO: In each sentence below there is a comma split. In the spaces below each sentence are the numbers of all the commas in the sentence. Find the comma split and write its number in the space at the left. Write what it is splitting beside that comma's number below the sentence. Next to the other numbers, write the buzzword of the comma rule for that comma.

__**2**__ (2) 1. Well, my pet shop trip was, an interesting, moving experience.
(commas numbered 1, 2, 3)

__ (1) #1 *introductory single word*

__ (1) #2 *splits linking verb and complement*

__ (1) #3 *two adjectives "and test"*

__**1**__ (2) 2. All the little animals, had sweet faces, cuddly bodies, and huge eyes.
(commas numbered 1, 2, 3)

__ (1) #1 *splits subject and verb*

__ (1) #2 *items in a series*

__ (1) #3 *items in a series*

__**3**__ (2) 3. From the bottom of my heart, I wanted to adopt them all, but my mom said, no.
(commas numbered 1, 2, 3)

__ (1) #1 *two+ intro prep phrases*

__ (1) #2 *compound sentence*

__ (1) #3 *splits verb and direct object*

Score Range		Result
25 - 23	=	Mastery
22 - 20	=	Superiority
19 - 18	=	Competency
17 - 15	=	Probationary
14 and below	=	Repeat

===
15

COMMAS: INTERRUPTERS

In this unit, as in the last one, we're going to be learning two comma rules. In the last unit you had two things which were set off by commas because they came at the beginning of the sentence. In *this* unit the comma rules you'll be learning will be about things that are "set off" by commas just because *they are what they are*; it doesn't matter whether they come at the beginning, the end, or the middle of a sentence.

When we say "set off," we mean that there are either commas before, after, or all around the interrupter, depending on where the interrupter is in the sentence. We'll show you several examples below, so you can see what we mean.

I. The buzzword for this rule is *"Direct Address."*

Direct address is when you are speaking to someone and you use their name (or a nickname or whatever) in the sentence. Look at the examples below to see how the direct address is set off by commas.

James, where do you think you're going?
Where, James, do you think you're going?
Where do you think you're going, James?

You could substitute a nickname (Sweetie, Slugger, Pookie Pie) or another form of address (old pal, my dear Mr. Smith, my fellow students), but you would still "set off" the direct address by commas.

II. *The buzzword for this rule is "Expressions."*

We use a lot of expressions in our language, such as *for example, by the way, on the other hand, therefore, in other words*. We use them to sort of help the person listening to us know which way our thinking is going.

There's a reason I won't let you go in the pool now. For example, you just ate a big meal.

Do you see how the *for example* lets you know what's coming up in the next sentence? You could also write the same sentence like this:

You just, for example, ate a big meal.
You just ate a big meal, for example.

INTERRUPTERS: EXERCISE #1

NAME: ____

WHAT TO DO: In each sentence, insert the commas where they should go.

1. Lucas, have you written your thank you notes for the birthday gifts you got?

2. You did, after all, get a fantastic new video game from Nana.

3. I can't find a good pen, Mom.

4. By the way, can you find me Nana's address?

5. I put all that stuff on the desk in your room last night, dear.

WHAT TO DO: Copy-edit the errors in the following sentences. There are five errors.

I got all my thank you notes written last night. I sat right down at my desk, got out my paper and pen and got to work. Yes it seems like a lot of work but it really is important to thank people when they give you a gift. I really feel good when I get my thank you notes written and mailed.

(over)

WHAT TO DO: In each sentence below there is a comma split. In the spaces below each sentence are the numbers of all the commas in the sentence. Find the comma split and write its number in the space at the left. Write what it is splitting beside that comma's number below the sentence. Next to the other numbers, write the buzzword of the comma rule for that comma.

1 1. For my eighth, birthday I got a bike, a skateboard, and a couple of great new video games.
(commas: 1, 2, 3)

#1 *splits noun and its modifier*

#2 *items in a series*

#3 *items in a series*

1 2. My favorite, is my shiny new bike which, by the way, I've been wanting forever!
(commas: 1, 2, 3)

#1 *splits subject and verb*

#2 *expressions*

#3 *expressions*

2 3. At the end of our road, we have an empty lot where the guys in the neighborhood have built, a bike track.
(commas: 1, 2)

#1 *two+ intro prep phrases*

#2 *splits verb and direct object*

INTERRUPTERS: EXERCISE #2

NAME: ____

WHAT TO DO: In each sentence, insert the commas where they should go.

1. Oh boy, my little sister is having her birthday next week.

2. Sarah, what theme did you choose for your party?

3. A princess theme, I'm sure, is something your friends will like.

4. Pink and purple are not my favorites, little sis.

5. If I chose the colors, on the other hand, they'd be orange and blue.

WHAT TO DO: Copy-edit the errors in the following sentences. There are five errors.

I want to go to my sister's party, and help her celebrate. There will be cake, balloons, and party games. I am, most excited about the cake! I don't mind playing the little kid games, but I hope I don't have to wear a silly, party hat.

WHAT TO DO: In each sentence below there is a comma split. In the spaces below each sentence are the numbers of all the commas in the sentence. Find the comma split and write its number in the space at the left. Write what it is splitting beside that comma's number below the sentence. Next to the other numbers, write the buzzword of the comma rule for that comma.

1 1. I saved, my money to buy Sarah a beautiful, delicate doll.
1 2

#1 *splits verb and direct object*

#2 *two adjectives "and test"*

2 2. Oh, I, was so excited to give it to her, and I made sure to wrap the present with care.
1 2 3

#1 *introductory single word*

#2 *splits subject and verb*

#3 *compound sentence*

3 3. She opened the gift, my friend, and her, eyes lit up!
1 2 3

#1 *direct address*

#2 *direct address*

#3 *splits noun and its modifier*

INTERRUPTERS: EXERCISE #3

NAME: ____

WHAT TO DO: In each sentence, insert the commas where they should go.

1. Now, my little friend, is the time to write your thank you notes.

2. Just to be clear, wouldn't you like to be thanked for the gifts you give?

3. Get some cards with princesses on them, little sister.

4. How many cards do you need to write, for heaven's sake?

5. If you have that many cards, buddy, we'll divide them up over a few days to get them finished.

WHAT TO DO: Copy-edit the errors in the following sentences. There are five errors.

Any task is easier if you divide it up into easy, doable steps. You may have forty notes to write, but breaking that into five notes a day makes it easier to do. It is, important to say "thank you" to people who gave a gift. I always make a list, write a note, and check it off. The job, is more fun that way!

WHAT TO DO: In each sentence below there is a comma split. In the spaces below each sentence are the numbers of all the commas in the sentence. Find the comma split and write its number in the space at the left. Write what it is splitting beside that comma's number below the sentence. Next to the other numbers, write the buzzword of the comma rule for that comma.

1 1. I helped, my sister make a fun, colorful chart to track her notes.
(commas numbered: 1 after "helped," 2 after "fun,")

#1 *splits verb and direct object*

#2 *two adjectives "and test"*

1 2. She, wrote five thank you notes, and I rewarded her with a star on the chart.
(commas numbered: 1 after "She," 2 after "notes,")

#1 *splits subject and verb*

#2 *compound sentence*

2 3. Well, those notes, were written in no time at all!
(commas numbered: 1 after "Well," 2 after "notes,")

#1 *introductory single word*

#2 *splits subject and verb*

TEST: INTERRUPTERS

NAME: ______________________________

POINTS EARNED:__________ out of 29 ______ LEVEL: ____________________

WHAT TO DO: In each sentence, insert the commas where they should go. If the sentence is correct as written, just leave it blank.

__ / 1 1. My friends it is easy to put off writing thank you notes.

__ / 1 2. Of course you can always make a quick phone call.

__ / 2 3. You my computer whiz can even send an email.

__ / 2 4. Phone calls and emails however lack the personal touch.

__ / 2 5. Do you remember by any chance your big smile the last time you got a personal letter in the mail?

=== / 8

WHAT TO DO: Copy-edit the errors in the following sentences. There are five errors.

__ / 5

The mail comes to my house in the late, afternoon. I always run out, open the mailbox and grab the mail. Right on top was a bright yellow envelope and it was addressed to me! On the back of the envelope I saw my little niece's return address. I got a huge grin on my face when I, saw her thank you note!

(over)

=== / 13

WHAT TO DO: In each sentence below there is a comma split. In the spaces below each sentence are the numbers of all the commas in the sentence. Find the comma split and write its number in the space at the left. Write what it is splitting beside that comma's number below the sentence. Next to the other numbers, write the buzzword of the comma rule for that comma.

__**2**__ (2)

1. Hey, what did you get for your, birthday from from Grandma, Madeleine?
   (commas numbered 1, 2, 3)

__ (1) #1 *introductory single word*

__ (1) #2 *splits noun and its modifier*

__ (1) #3 *direct address*

__**1**__ (2)

2. She, sent me a soft, warm winter jacket, but it's too big.
   (commas numbered 1, 2, 3)

__ (1) #1 *splits subject and verb*

__ (1) #2 *two adjectives "and test"*

__ (1) #3 *compound sentence*

__**4**__ (2)

3. By the beginning of winter, I'll grow into it, of course, and it'll be, great!
   (commas numbered 1, 2, 3, 4)

__ (1) #1 *two+ intro prep phrases*

__ (1) #2 *expressions*

__ (1) #3 *expressions*

__ (1) #4 *splits linking verb and complement*

Score Range		Result
29 - 26	=	Mastery
25 - 23	=	Superiority
22 - 20	=	Competency
19 - 17	=	Probationary
16 and below	=	Repeat

===
16

COMMAS: NAMES, DATES, AND PLACES

We are about to learn our last comma rules. There are times in sentences when we have to talk about places, dates, and people's names. There are special rules for commas in some of these situations.

I. The buzzword for this rule is *"Names and Abbreviations."*

Do you know anyone who is named after someone else in his or her family? Some families have the tradition of passing down names from one generation to the next. Many times this results in people having something like Jr., Sr., or III after their names. Other times people have additions to their names when they earn a special degree at a university or college. In this case you'll see M.D. (medical doctor), Esq. (lawyers), or Ph.D. (doctor of philosophy) after that person's name.

You will put a comma between the name and the Jr., Sr., M.D., Ph.D., etc. The only time you won't put a comma is between a name and a Roman numeral (I, IV, etc.). Here are some examples:

Robert Karl, Jr.	James Yoffe, M.D.	George Smith, Esq.
Henry V	William Clemons IV	Thomas Jones, Ph.D.

II. The buzzword for this rule is *"Dates and Addresses."*

When we write out specific dates and addresses in sentences, there are particular comma rules we use. The commas are there to separate the different parts of the date or address. You DON'T use a comma between the month and date, the street number and the street, or between the state and zip code. Here are a few examples:

On January 20, 2008, we moved to 123 Main Street, Raleigh, North Carolina 27613.

My family moved to Raleigh, North Carolina, on Tuesday, January 20, 2008.

NOTE: When a date or address is part of a sentence, you must put a comma AFTER the last item, if the sentence continues on. Look at the comma after "North Carolina" and the one after "2008" in the sentences above. If the date or address doesn't contain a comma (such as: ... on January 20 I went ...) you don't put a comma after it.

COMMAS: NAMES, DATES, AND PLACES: EXERCISE #1

NAME: ____

WHAT TO DO: In each sentence, insert the commas where they should go.

1. I was born in Los Angeles, California, on January 20, 1974.

2. In 1981 my family and I moved to 2830 Chesapeake Avenue, Anchorage, Alaska 99516.

3. My family lived in Anchorage, Alaska, for many years.

4. After I graduated from high school on May 23, 1992, I left for college in Pullman, Washington.

5. The next year I switched schools and moved to Las Vegas, Nevada, to complete my college degree.

WHAT TO DO: Copy-edit the errors in the following sentences. There are five errors.

Living in Las Vegas, Nevada was a lot of fun! I was, a singing waitress there. On May, 19, 1997, I walked across the stage to receive the degree I had earned. That, was a great feeling! I will remember with fondness my exciting fun-filled time in college.

(over)

WHAT TO DO: In each sentence below there is a comma split. In the spaces below each sentence are the numbers of all the commas in the sentence. Find the comma split and write its number in the space at the left. Write what it is splitting beside that comma's number below the sentence. Next to the other numbers, write the buzzword of the comma rule for that comma.

1 1. I, went home to Anchorage, Alaska, in the summer of 1997.
(commas numbered 1, 2, 3)

#1 *splits subject and verb*

#2 *names, dates, & places*

#3 *names, dates, & places*

1 2. My address again became, 2830 Chesapeake Avenue, Anchorage, Alaska 99516.
(commas numbered 1, 2, 3)

#1 *splits linking verb and complement*

#2 *names, dates, & places*

#3 *names, dates, & places*

2 3. By the middle of May 1998, I was ready to follow in the footsteps of my, uncles and join the Air Force.
(commas numbered 1, 2)

#1 *2+ intro prep phrases*

#2 *splits modifier and its noun*

COMMAS: NAMES, DATES, AND PLACES: EXERCISE #2

NAME: ____

WHAT TO DO: In each sentence, insert the commas where they should go.

1. My oldest uncle's name is William Tell Clemons III.

2. His grandfather was William Tell Clemons Jr.

3. My uncle became a lawyer, and then he wrote his name as William Tell Clemons Esq.

4. This trend continued when I married my husband Robert Joseph Karl Jr.

5. We named our son Robert Joseph Karl III.

WHAT TO DO: Copy-edit the errors in the following sentences. There are five errors.

Both of my uncles, served in the Air Force. After college I was inspired to serve my country and I began to look around for a way to do that. I went to the library looked up all sorts of books on women in the military, and read for days on the subject. I shocked, my parents when I told them I had decided on the Air Force. To tell the truth they thought I was too "girlie" to be interested in such a career!

(over)

WHAT TO DO: In each sentence below there is a comma split. In the spaces below each sentence are the numbers of all the commas in the sentence. Find the comma split and write its number in the space at the left. Write what it is splitting beside that comma's number below the sentence. Next to the other numbers, write the buzzword of the comma rule for that comma.

1 1. My decision to join to Air Force, (1) was one of the best, (2) most important decisions of my life.

#1 *splits subject and verb*

#2 *two adjectives "and" test*

3 2. I learned discipline, (1) acquired leadership skills, (2) and developed a deep, (3) love of my country.

#1 *items in a series*

#2 *items in a series*

#3 *splits modifier and its noun*

1 3. My first duty station was, (1) Cape Canaveral, (2) Florida, (3) where they launch the space shuttles.

#1 *splits linking verb and complement*

#2 *names, dates, & places*

#3 *names, dates, & places*

COMMAS: NAMES, DATES, AND PLACES: EXERCISE #3

NAME: ____

WHAT TO DO: In each sentence, insert the commas where they should go. If the sentence is correct as written, just leave it blank.

1. My husband's father's name is Robert Joseph Karl Sr.
2. On June 30 2003 he retired from his engineering job and moved to 301 Palm Avenue Miami Florida.
3. He and his wife love to play with Robert Joseph Karl III.
4. We've given him the nickname "Tripp," and he livens up our lives at 7615 Vista del Rey Lane Raleigh North Carolina.
5. Maybe someday Tripp will grow up to be Robert Joseph Karl M.D.

WHAT TO DO: Copy-edit the errors in the following sentences. There are five errors.

Right now Tripp's favorite thing in the whole world is, Thomas the Train. As a matter of fact he even has Thomas the Train pajamas! On the floor in the living room he loves to set up his train tracks and play with all his trains. We can usually get him to eat, his vegetables if we pretend that they are Thomas' green train friends. Tripp here comes Thomas' little green engine buddy named Percy!

WHAT TO DO: In each sentence below there is a comma split. In the spaces below each sentence are the numbers of all the commas in the sentence. Find the comma split and write its number in the space at the left. Write what it is splitting beside that comma's number below the sentence. Next to the other numbers, write the buzzword of the comma rule for that comma.

3 1. Class, today we are going to learn about the ancient, time honored, traditions having to do with names.
(commas numbered 1, 2, 3)

#1 *direct address*

#2 *two adjectives "and" test*

#3 *splits modifier and its noun*

2 2. For many years in our history, we have given boys, the names of their fathers, but there are certain rules.
(commas numbered 1, 2, 3)

#1 *2+ intro prep phrases*

#2 *splits indirect object and direct object*

#3 *compound sentence*

2 3. Yes, a comma, goes between a name and an abbreviation but not between a name and a Roman numeral.
(commas numbered 1, 2)

#1 *introductory single word*

#2 *splits subject and verb*

TEST: COMMAS: NAMES, DATES, AND PLACES

NAME: ______________________________

POINTS EARNED: ________ out of 29 ________ LEVEL: ____________________

WHAT TO DO: In each sentence, insert the commas where they should go. If the sentence is correct as written, just leave it blank.

__ 1 1. The present queen of England is Elizabeth II.

__ 1 2. My nephew's name is George Clinton, Jr., and he's an expert on English royalty.

__ 2 3. Queen Elizabeth's main address is Buckingham Palace, London, England.

__ 2 4. On June 3, 2010, he was able to see the Queen's house up close when he went to England on a trip.

__ 3 5. He stayed in England until June 17, 2010, and then he returned home to 150 Elm Circle, Birmingham, Alabama.

WHAT TO DO: Copy-edit the errors in the following sentences. There are five errors.

My favorite English king is Henry VIII, but he wasn't a very nice man. The most famous thing about him is, his six wives. His wives were Catharine of Aragon, Anne Boleyn, Jane Seymour, Anne of Cleves, Katherine Howard, and Catherine Parr. His first three wives went through great, painful struggles to give the king a son. There was a great, celebration when his son Edward was born.

__ 5

=== 14

(over)

WHAT TO DO: In each sentence below there is a comma split. In the spaces below each sentence are the numbers of all the commas in the sentence. Find the comma split and write its number in the space at the left. Write what it is splitting beside that comma's number below the sentence. Next to the other numbers, write the buzzword of the comma rule for that comma.

__ **2** (2)

1. Students, today our lesson, is about Anne Boleyn, and she was Henry VIII's second wife.
   (commas numbered 1, 2, 3)

__ #1 (1) *direct address*

__ #2 (1) *splits subject and verb*

__ #3 (1) *compound sentence*

__ **2** (2)

2. To say the least, her personal goal was to fulfill the king's most heartfelt, wish to have a son.
   (commas numbered 1, 2)

__ #1 (1) *expressions*

__ #2 (1) *splits modifier and its noun*

__ **2** (2)

3. No, she was, unable to have a Henry, Jr., but she did give birth to England's greatest queen named Elizabeth I.
   (commas numbered 1, 2, 3, 4)

__ #1 (1) *introductory single word*

__ #2 (1) *splits linking verb and complement*

__ #3 (1) *names, dates, & places*

__ #4 (1) *compound sentence*

Score Range		Result
29 - 26	=	Mastery
25 - 23	=	Superiority
22 - 20	=	Competency
19 - 17	=	Probationary
16 and below	=	Repeat

__ (15)

DIRECT QUOTATIONS

When you're reading something, how do you know who is saying what?

"Bill, I want to go home," said John.

The "buzz word" for this will be "direct quote."

In the sentence above, who is speaking? John! Right!

In English we use punctuation called quotation marks to show when words are being spoken by someone in particular.

What about in this sentence:

"John, I was hoping to stay a little longer," I said.

Assuming these two sentences form a little story, who is speaking now? That's right ... Bill!

These ---> " " <--- are QUOTATION MARKS. You always put them around the words people speak. Whatever is inside the quotation marks (words and punctuation) is called DIALOGUE. The rest of the sentence (*said John* or *I said*) is called the NARRATIVE. The narrative tells us who is speaking and sometimes gives us more information about what is happening. Here's another example:

As I walked in the room, I yelled, "Is anyone here?"

Now, there are a few specific things to know when using quotation marks. Pay attention to these examples and look back at them during your exercises if you need help.

A. Always begin your dialogue with a capital letter if the quote is a sentence.

James said, "Tell me more about your trip."

B. The BROKEN QUOTE: When a quoted sentence of *dialogue is divided into two parts with narrative in between*, the second part of the dialogue begins with a lower case letter.

"I really was hoping,"said Pam, "that you would come."

C. Sometimes the speaker has more than one sentence to say. Here's an example:

"The state fair is great!" cried Janie. "Don't you want to go? I do!"

Each time you write dialogue, *you must enclose the entire speech in quotation marks*, even if the dialogue consists of fourteen sentences! Please also note that when you have a complete sentence in front of the narrative, you must have a period after the narrative. So this is different from the broken quote we described in part B of these notes.

D. Suppose you are writing a sentence which begins with dialogue and ends with narrative. And then suppose that your dialogue is a statement, which would ordinarily end with a period. Here's how you might think it should be done:

"I wish I could go to the state fair." said Bob.

Now, I think that sentence looks confusing. We know that a period is a signal to the reader to come to a full stop, right? So, if the reader comes to a full stop after *fair*, then is he supposed to come to another full stop after *Bob*?

Here's how we solve this problem: we change the period after *fair* to a comma, so it looks like this:

"I wish I could go to the state fair," said Bob.

Now it's not confusing at all! We only do this if the punctuation would have been a period. If it is an exclamation mark or question mark, you leave it there.

E. When you go from dialogue to narrative or narrative to dialogue - *unless there is other punctuation present* - you need a comma to "change gears" from one to the other.

I asked, "Who is your science teacher?"
(note the location of the comma after "asked")

The "buzz word" for this will be "change gear comma"

"He is my favorite science teacher!" yelled Roger.
(note there is no "change gear" comma because there is an exclamation mark)

The buzzword for this comma is *gear change comma.*

The buzzword for quotation marks is *quotation marks*.

When copy editing, insert quotation marks and capitalize words like this:

I said, this is my quote.

DIRECT QUOTATIONS: EXERCISE #1

NAME: ____

WHAT TO DO: In this exercise we have put in all the punctuation needed *except* the quotation marks. Read each sentence below carefully and insert the quotation marks where you think they should go.

1. Bobby looked at his best friend Jason and asked, "Do you ever think about being a grownup?"

2. "Yeah," said Jason. "It's kind of scary, isn't it?"

3. "There's a lot to learn," said Bobby. "You have to learn about money, for example. Do you ever save money?"

4. "My mom and dad pay me for doing my chores," said Jason, "but I have to save one-third of it for college and one-third of it for gifts. I get to spend the rest on whatever I want."

5. "That's a good idea!" exclaimed Bobby. "I think I'll talk to my mom and dad about that."

WHAT TO DO: Copy-edit the errors in the following sentences. There are five errors. *From now on each set of quotation marks counts as one thing.*

Tripp and Maddie, are too young to learn about saving money, but in a year from now Maddie will begin to learn about saving. She's still learning the difference between pennies, nickles, dimes and quarters. Once I gave her, three pennies and I had a quarter. She said, "I have more monies than you do!"

WHAT TO DO: In each sentence below there is a comma split. In the spaces below each sentence are the numbers of all the other punctuation in the sentence. Find the comma split and write its number in the space at the left. Write what it is splitting beside that comma's number below the sentence. Next to the other numbers, write the buzzword of the comma rule for that comma and identify the other punctuation. Remember that each set of quotation marks counts as one thing. We will only put a number under the open quote (") mark, not the close quote (") mark.

1 1. Maddie's first, chores will be putting her toys away,
1 2
making her bed, and setting the table.
3

#1 *splits modifier and its noun*

#2 *items in a series*

#3 *items in a series*

2 2. Yes, Maddie must do, all her chores, and she'll be
1 2 3
paid one dollar a day.

#1 *introductory single word*

#2 *splits verb and direct object*

#3 *compound sentence*

1 3. At day's end she, must put away her toys after
1
I've said only once, "Maddie, put your toys away."
2 3

#1 *splits subject and verb*

#2 *gear change comma*

#3 *quotation marks*

DIRECT QUOTATIONS: EXERCISE #2

NAME: ____

WHAT TO DO: In this exercise you must put in all the punctuation needed along with the quotation marks. Read each sentence below carefully and insert the punctuation where you think it should go.

1. Bobby said, "Hey, Jason, I talked to my parents about being paid for my chores."

2. "Well, what did they say?" asked Jason.

3. "They said we'd start the whole program next Monday," said Bobby.

4. "What will your chores be?" asked Jason.

5. "I have to make my bed, put my dirty clothes in the hamper, hang up my clean clothes, and clear the table after dinner," said Jason as the two boys began to ride their bikes.

WHAT TO DO: Copy-edit the errors in the following sentences. There are five errors. *From now on each set of quotation marks counts as one thing.*

Bobby, needless to say, knows the value of the different coins and bills. He is an older boy than Maddie. He has four chores to do each day, and he must do them without having to be told more than one time. He will begin his savings program on Friday, September 15, 2011. Each Friday his dad will give him 34 cents for spending and 66 cents to be divided into his college and gift savings accounts.

(over)

WHAT TO DO: In each sentence below there is a comma split. Find the comma split and write its number in the space at the left. Write what it is splitting beside that comma's number below the sentence. Next to the other numbers, write the buzzword of the comma rule for that comma and identify the other punctuation. Remember that each set of quotation marks counts as one thing. We will only put a number under the open quote mark, not the close quote mark.

1 1. On Friday Bobby looked at the 34, cents in his hand
1
and said, "That doesn't look like very much!"
2 3

#1 *splits modifier and its noun*

#2 *gear change comma*

#3 *quotation marks*

4 2. "That's true," said Dad, "but at the the of the month
1 2 3
you'll have, $1.65 to spend."
4

#1 *quotation marks*

#2 *gear change comma*

#3 *quotation marks*

#4 *splits verb and direct object*

1 3. Bobby, stared at the money in his hand and said,
1 2
"Dad, think of what I'll have in savings at the end
3 4
of the YEAR!"

#1 *splits subject and verb*

#2 *gear change comma*

#3 *quotation marks*

#4 *direct address*

DIRECT QUOTATIONS: EXERCISE #3

NAME: ______________________________

WHAT TO DO: In this exercise you must put in all the punctuation needed along with the quotation marks. Read each sentence below carefully and insert the punctuation and capitalization where you think it should go. If a letter needs to be capitalized, draw three short lines underneath it.

1. Six months after they had started the program, Bobby said to Jason, "I have almost ten dollars to spend on Craig's birthday gift."

2. "Wow!" exclaimed Jason. "How'd you manage that?"

3. "Remember how my parents and I started my savings program?" asked Bobby. "I've got the money all saved up."

4. "And another neat thing," said Bobby, "is that by the end of the year I'll have almost twenty dollars in my college account."

5. Jason said, "My parents say that as I get older my chores will increase and so will the money I get paid so both my savings accounts will grow even more."

WHAT TO DO: Copy-edit the errors in the following sentences. There are five errors. *From now on each set of quotation marks counts as one thing.*

Bobby's grandfather would always give him, a ten dollar bill every time he came for a visit. He would always say "Bobby, remember that money doesn't grow on trees." Bobby was, proud when he told his grandfather what he was learning about money.

WHAT TO DO: In each sentence below there is a comma split. Find the comma split and write its number in the space at the left. Write what it is splitting beside that comma's number below the sentence. Next to the other numbers, write the buzzword of the comma rule for that comma and identify the other punctuation. Remember that each set of quotation marks counts as one thing. We will only put a number under the open quote mark, not the close quote mark.

3 1. Bobby's grandfather lives in Madison,(1) Wisconsin,(2) and he only gets to visit every six,(3) months or so.

#1 *names, dates, & places*

#2 *compound sentence*

#3 *splits modifier and its noun*

1 2. His grandfather's name,(1) is Robert Carl Madison,(2) Sr.

#1 *splits subject and verb*

#2 *names, dates, & places*

1 3. Bobby's dad is,(1) Robert Carl Madison, Jr.,(2) and,(3) of course,(4) Bobby is Robert Carl Madison III.

#1 *splits linking verb and complement*

#2 *compound sentence*

#3 *expressions*

#4 *expressions*

TEST: DIRECT QUOTATIONS

NAME: ______________________________

POINTS EARNED: ________ out of 54 ____ LEVEL: ______________

WHAT TO DO: In each sentence, insert all punctuation and capitalization where it should go. If a letter needs to be capitalized, draw three short lines underneath it. If the sentence is correct as written, just leave it blank.

__/5 1. Bobby's grandfather asked, "How did you learn so much about money?"

__/7 2. "I have chores to do every day," answered Bobby, "and I get paid a dollar a day for doing them."

__/8 3. "A dollar a day is a lot of money!" exclaimed Grandpa. "Do you spend it all on bubble gum and candy?"

__/7 4. "No, Grandpa," said Bobby, "I have to save one-third for college and one-third for gifts. As I get older, I'll have more chores and get paid more money."

__/7 5. "That's a very good plan," said Grandpa. "I'm proud of you." *

WHAT TO DO: Copy-edit the errors in the following sentences. There are five errors.

__/5 "Bobby, you've really learned a lot about money," said Grandpa. At the end of Grandpa's visit, Bobby had done his chores, received his money, and added to his savings accounts. His grandfather was extremely proud of Bobby.

===
39

*could also be !"

WHAT TO DO: In each sentence below there is a comma split. Find the comma split and write its number in the space at the left. Write what it is splitting beside that comma's number below the sentence. Next to the other numbers, write the buzzword of the comma rule for that comma and identify the other punctuation. Remember that each set of quotation marks counts as one thing. We will only put a number under the open quote mark, not the close quote mark.

__ / 2 **1** 1. Money, knowledg should be a part of every student's schooling, or he might make expensive mistakes later in life.
(1: comma after "Money"; 2: comma after "schooling")

__ / 1 #1 *splits modifier and its noun*

__ / 1 #2 *compound sentence*

__ / 2 **3** 2. "Dad, I've decided that I will always save, a certain portion of the money I make," said Bobby.
(1: open quote; 2: comma after "Dad"; 3: comma after "save"; 4: comma after "make")

__ / 1 #1 *quotation marks*

__ / 1 #2 *direct address*

__ / 1 #3 *splits verb and direct object*

__ / 1 #4 *gear change comma*

__ / 2 **3** 3. In a special piggy bank in his room, Bobby kept his college savings, and he kept his gift savings account in a leather, wallet in his dresser.
(1: comma after "room"; 2: comma after "savings"; 3: comma after "leather")

__ / 1 #1 *2+ intro prep phrases*

__ / 1 #2 *compound sentence*

__ / 1 #3 *splits modifier and its noun*

=== / 15

Score Range		Result
54 - 49	=	Mastery
48 - 43	=	Superiority
42 - 38	=	Competency
37 - 32	=	Probationary
31 and below	=	Repeat

TITLES

Books, magazines, plays, and movies all have titles. Do you remember reading Good Night Moon or Hop on Pop when you were little? When we use the titles of things in sentences, we underline, italicize, or use quotation marks to show the title. We also capitalize them differently. If we don't, it can be confusing.

Let's say there was a book about furniture called The Living Room.

I was reading yesterday in the living room that red couches are popular.

Are you talking about the book or were you actually in the living room when you were reading? That's why it's important to be clear:

I was reading yesterday in The Living Room that red couches are popular.

So, how do you know what to underline and what to put in quotation marks? It has to do with ***size***. Take a look at these two columns:

Underline	Quotation Marks
Books	Chapters
Newspapers	Newspaper articles
CDs	Songs
Movies	TV or Radio shows
Plays	Poems
Magazines	Magazine articles

Do you see how major (larger) works get underlined and minor (smaller) works get quotation marks? Here are a couple of examples:

In USA Today there was an article called "The Schooling Game" that talked about different schools around the country.

Have you read the chapter called "The Piano Lesson" in that book How to Be a Musician?

The "buzzword" for this rule is "titles."

NOTE: You may see titles that would normally be underlined set off in *italics* instead. It's the same thing. If you're ever typing on a computer and have a major work, you can use *italics*, too.

TITLES: EXERCISE #1

NAME: ______________________________

WHAT TO DO: In the sentences below there are certain titles. Put quotation marks around the ones that need quotation marks, and underline the ones that need to be underlined.

1. My book Adventures in Neverland was due at the library.
2. When I went to the library to return it, the librarian was reading a story called "How To Say No to a Monster."
3. After the story she read one of my favorite poems called "Jabberwocky."
4. Then, after choosing different parts to read, we read a play called Anne Meets Gilbert.
5. Finally we heard a new CD by Kermit the Frog called Being Nice to Green Things.

WHAT TO DO: Copy-edit the errors in the following sentences. There are five errors.

Well, I just love to go to the library! Our local one is at 425 Elm Street, Middleboro, Ohio. My idea of a great day, is to check out a stack of books, bring them home to my room, and read through them when I'm all alone. In a cozy corner of my bedroom, there's a comfortable, chair that's my favorite spot for reading.

WHAT TO DO: In each sentence below there is a comma split. In the spaces below each sentence are the numbers of all the other punctuation in the sentence. Find the comma split and write its number in the space at the left. Write what it is splitting beside that comma's number below the sentence. Next to the other numbers, write the buzzword of the rule for that punctuation. Remember that each set of quotation marks counts as one thing. We will only put a number under the open quote (") mark, not the close quote (") mark.

1 1. The lady at our local library, always says, "Remember
1 2 3
to keep your voice down in the reading section."

#1 *splits subject and verb*

#2 *gear change comma*

#3 *quotation marks*

2 2. During my trip to the library, I usually pick, one
1 2
thrilling, spine-tingling mystery book.
3

#1 *2+ intro prep phrases*

#2 *splits verb and direct object*

#3 *two adjectives "and" test*

1 3. The latest mystery book I read was, The Case of
1
the Hidden Birdcage, and I read it all in one
2 3
afternoon!

#1 *splits linking verb and complement*

#2 *titles*

#3 *compound sentence*

TITLES: EXERCISE #2

NAME: ____

WHAT TO DO: In the sentences below there are certain titles. Put quotation marks around the ones that need quotation marks, and underline the ones that need to be underlined.

1. Last Saturday my buddies and I went to see the new movie The New Adventures of the Hulk.

2. It is based on the story "Hulk Strikes Again."

3. You can find that story in the magazine Everyday Superheroes.

4. After the movie we were all singing the theme song "Hulk Saves the Day."

5. I'm going to buy the CD called Songs for Superheroes.

WHAT TO DO: Copy-edit the errors in the following sentences. There are five errors.

My mom said, "Kevin you've been singing that song all day. It's driving me crazy! I gave my mom, an apologetic look and told her that I'd really try to stop. With a huge effort on my part I managed to stop singing the song for about fifteen minutes, but then it just, popped out of my mouth!

(over)

WHAT TO DO: In each sentence below there is a comma split. In the spaces below each sentence are the numbers of all the other punctuation in the sentence. Find the comma split and write its number in the space at the left. Write what it is splitting beside that comma's number below the sentence. Next to the other numbers, write the buzzword of the rule for that punctuation. Remember that each set of quotation marks counts as one thing. We will only put a number under the open quote (") mark, not the close quote (") mark.

1 1. Kevin loves to pretend that he is, (1) a superhero, (2) but his little sister Marie loves beautiful, (3) magical princesses.

#1 *splits linking verb and complement*

#2 *compound sentence*

#3 *two adjectives "and" test*

2 2. Marie has a CD called Singing Princesses (1) with all her favorite, (2) songs about Cinderella, (3) Snow White, (4) and Sleeping Beauty.

#1 *titles*

#2 *splits modifier and its noun*

#3 *items in a series*

#4 *items in a series*

2 3. Marie is "all girl" and Kevin is "all boy," (1) but their best, (2) times together can be with a couple of old cardboard boxes!

#1 *compound sentence*

#2 *splits modifier and its noun*

TITLES: EXERCISE #3

NAME: ______________________________

WHAT TO DO: In the sentences below there are certain titles. Put quotation marks around the ones that need quotation marks, and underline the ones that need to be underlined.

1. Last Saturday afternoon I decided to re-read my favorite book Mrs. Piggle-Wiggle.

2. My favorite story in that book is called "The Selfishness Cure."

3. Then I read one of my favorite poems called "Casey at the Bat."

4. That poem gave me the idea to read the sports section of our local newspaper The Daily Gazette.

5. Reading about last night's baseball game made me want to sing the old song "Take Me Out to the Ballgame."

WHAT TO DO: Copy-edit the errors in the following sentences. There are five errors.

My uncle, James Patterson Wilson, Jr., played minor league baseball when he was, a young man. He was the star pitcher, as a matter of fact, of the Danville Devils. He loves to tell, the story of the time he hit the winning homerun in the final series game. Yes, he will remember that day always!

(over)

WHAT TO DO: In each sentence below there is a comma split. In the spaces below each sentence are the numbers of all the other punctuation in the sentence. Find the comma split and write its number in the space at the left. Write what it is splitting beside that comma's number below the sentence. Next to the other numbers, write the buzzword of the rule for that punctuation. Remember that each set of quotation marks counts as one thing. We will only put a number under the open quote (") mark, not the close quote (") mark.

2 1. The poem "Casey at the Bat" is about the last, inning of a baseball game with two outs, two strikes, and bases loaded.
(1 = "Casey at the Bat"; 2 = last,; 3 = outs,; 4 = strikes,)

#1 *titles*

#2 *splits modifier and its noun*

#3 *items in a series*

#4 *items in a series*

2 2. Proud, arrogant Casey, walked slowly up to the plate to take his turn at bat.
(1 = Proud,; 2 = Casey,)

#1 *two adjectives "and" test*

#2 *splits subject and verb*

1 3. Everything, depended on Casey's getting a hit, but you must read the poem to find out what happened.
(1 = Everything,; 2 = hit,)

#1 *splits subject and verb*

#2 *compound sentence*

TEST: TITLES

NAME: ____

POINTS EARNED:__________ out of 25 ________ LEVEL: __________________

WHAT TO DO: In the sentences below there are certain titles. Put quotation marks around the ones that need quotation marks, and underline the ones that need to be underlined.

__ 1. Another of my favorite books is Mary Poppins.
1

__ 2. I always love to re-read the chapter called "Bird Woman."
1

__ 3. Disney made a wonderful movie about Mary Poppins, and she sang a beautiful song called "Feed the Birds."
1

__ 4. Jane and Michael's father Mr. Banks was always getting angry and writing letters to their newspaper, the London Times.
1

__ 5. In the end, however, the whole family was happy when they sang "Let's Go Fly a Kite."
1

WHAT TO DO: Copy-edit the errors in the following sentences. There are five errors.

In the book called Mary Poppins the Banks family consisted of Mr. and Mrs. Banks, Jane, Michael, and twin babies. They advertised for a new nanny to work at their house at 2 Cherry Tree Lane, London, England. After she said firmly, "I make it a rule never to give references," Mary Poppins slid UP the banister! Jane and Michael knew that this nanny was someone very special.

__
5

===
10

(over)

WHAT TO DO: In each sentence below there is a comma split. In the spaces below each sentence are the numbers of all the other punctuation in the sentence. Find the comma split and write its number in the space at the left. Write what it is splitting beside that comma's number below the sentence. Next to the other numbers, write the buzzword of the rule for that punctuation. Remember that each set of quotation marks counts as one thing. We will only put a number under the open quote (") mark, not the close quote (") mark.

__ **2** __ (2 points)

1. On the day of their first outing,[1] Mary Poppins,[2] took Jane and Michael to visit Uncle Albert in a chapter called "[3]Laughing Gas."

__ (1) #1 *2+ intro prep phrases*

__ (1) #2 *splits subject and verb*

__ (1) #3 *titles*

__ **2** __ (2 points)

2. Well,[1] Uncle Albert,[2] was a fat,[3] jolly old man who was floating in the air of his parlor because it was his birthday.

__ (1) #1 *introductory single word*

__ (1) #2 *splits subject and verb*

__ (1) #3 *two adjectives "and" test*

__ **2** __ (2 points)

3. "[1]If I laugh on that particular,[2] day I become so filled with Laughing Gas that I simply can't keep on the ground,[3]" said Uncle Albert.

__ (1) #1 *quotation marks*

__ (1) #2 *splits modifier and its noun*

__ (1) #3 *gear change comma*

=== 15 90

Score Range		Result
25 - 22	=	Mastery
21 - 20	=	Superiority
19 - 17	=	Competency
16 - 15	=	Probationary
14 and below	=	Repeat

POSSESSIVES

Think of your most treasured possession. What is it? A toy? A trophy? A family heirloom? I know a little girl named Maddie, and her prized possession is her stuffed pony.

Maddie has a stuffed pony in her room.

What's another way we can say that Maddie REALLY owns that pony?

Maddie's stuffed pony is in her room.

Right! We turned Maddie into a possessive by adding an apostrophe with an S ('s) to the end of it. Now we all know who the pony belongs to.

Here are some other examples of possessives:

The brown dog's bark was very loud.
My aunt's apple pie is the best!
Our home's porch needs a coat of paint.

Now, we have to be careful that we don't use an 's to make something plural instead of possessive. Here are the same three examples used as plurals:

The brown dogs all walked in our yard.
All my aunts came to visit for the wedding.
We all put Christmas lights on our homes.

We use plurals when we mean more than one of something. We use possessives to show ownership of something. They're very different, so we have to make sure we don't get them mixed up:

Plural	Possessive
cats	cat's
girls	girl's
cabinets	cabinet's

If we were to see the words below before a noun, we'd label them as adjectives, but sometimes they're called *possessive pronouns*. We don't need an 's on these ... they're already in their possessive form.

his/hers/its* mine/ours yours/theirs/whose/your

**Especially "its." NO apostrophe.*

The "buzzword" for this punctuation is *"possessives."*

POSSESSIVES: EXERCISE #1

NAME: ____

WHAT TO DO: Some of the underlined portions in the sentences below are examples of PLURALS (PL), and some of them are examples of POSSESSIVES (PO). We have left the apostrophes off the possessives on purpose. Read the sentences carefully and decide if you have a plural or a possessive. Write PL in the space at the left if it's a plural and PO if it's a possessive.

PL 1. Some of the boys in my neighborhood played basketball after church.

PO 2. My friends basketball was in the best condition.

PO 3. They all played in Jasons driveway because it was the biggest.

PL 4. They organized themselves into two teams of four players each.

PO 5. After a hard-fought game the older players team was the winner!

WHAT TO DO: Some of the sentences below have PLURALS , and some of them have POSSESSIVES. Circle the correct form of the word (no apostrophe ['] for plurals and an apostrophe ['] for possessives) in each sentence.

1. After their defeat the younger (boys, boy's) decided they wanted a re-match.
2. We decided to practice in my (neighbors, neighbor's) driveway.
3. All the (neighbors, neighbor's) got excited about the re-match.
4. My best (friends, friend's) excellent shooting ability was going to be a plus!
5. Even the (girls, girl's) on our street starting to get into the fun.

(over)

WHAT TO DO: In each sentence below there is a comma split. In the spaces below each sentence are the numbers of all the other punctuation in the sentence. Find the comma split and write its number in the space at the left. Write what it is splitting beside that comma's number below the sentence. Next to the other numbers, write the buzzword of the rule for that punctuation. Remember that each set of quotation marks counts as one thing. We will only put a number under the open quote (") mark, not the close quote (") mark.

2 1. Good, vigorous exercise, is one of the most important
(1 under "Good,"; 2 under "exercise,")
ways to keep our bodies healthy, but we often get lazy.
(3 under "healthy,")

#1 *two adjectives "and" test*

#2 *splits subject and verb*

#3 *compound sentence*

2 2. In my latest Highlights magazine the whole, theme
(1 under "Highlights"; 2 under "whole,")
was about exercise, games, and health.
(3 under "exercise,"; 4 under "games,")

#1 *titles*

#2 *splits modifier and its noun*

#3 *items in a series*

#4 *items in a series*

1 3. One writer wrote, a story about a boy's decision
(1 under "wrote,"; 2 under "boy's")
to get up off the couch and get daily exercise.

#1 *splits verb and direct object*

#2 *possessives*

POSSESSIVES: EXERCISE #2

NAME: ______________________________

WHAT TO DO: Circle the correct form of the word in the sentences below.

1. One (girls, girl's) favorite form of exercise is her ballet class.

2. If you watch (dancers, dancer's) on television, you can see that they are in top physical condition.

3. My other (friends, friend's) dance class includes ballet, jazz, and tap.

WHAT TO DO: All the sentences below contain possessives. Put the apostrophe ['] in the correct place.

1. The ballet teachers name is Miss Cindy.

2. She studied ballet at New Yorks famous Juilliard School of Music.

3. Miss Cindys dream was to be a ballerina, but she decided to teach instead.

WHAT TO DO: Copy-edit the errors in the following sentences. There are SIX errors.

Dad said, "Let's walk to the park today and get some exercise! We were all, excited about going to the park and we got our playclothes and running shoes on. I was determined to try out some new stretching exercises I had seen in a story called Get Your Body Ready from my latest Running magazine. I was sure I looked like a real, athlete in my new shoes and gear.

(over)

WHAT TO DO: In each sentence below there is a comma split. In the spaces below each sentence are the numbers of all the other punctuation in the sentence. Find the comma split and write its number in the space at the left. Write what it is splitting beside that comma's number below the sentence. Next to the other numbers, write the buzzword of the rule for that punctuation. Remember that each set of quotation marks counts as one thing. We will only put a number under the open quote (") mark, not the close quote (") mark.

2 1. At the beginning of vigorous exercise, it is a good idea
1
to stretch the muscles gently to avoid any, injury.
2

#1 *2+ intro prep phrases*

#2 *splits modifier and its noun*

3 2. Young children, on the other hand, do not need to
1 2
stretch, their muscles when they just go out to play.
3

#1 *expressions*

#2 *expressions*

#3 *splits verb and direct object*

2 3. My young friend, be sure to include, some
1 2
exercise in your day, or your body will grow weak.
3

#1 *direct address*

#2 *splits verb and direct object*

#3 *compound sentence*

POSSESSIVES: EXERCISE #3

NAME: ____

WHAT TO DO: All the sentences below contain possessives. Put the apostrophe ['] in the correct place.

1. All my bodys muscles are designed to do certain jobs.
2. My moms advice to me is always to get up and get moving.
3. On the weekends my dads idea is to get us involved in some physical game.
4. I usually try to overcome my big brothers height advantage by being quick.
5. My big sisters goal is to make as much noise as possible!

WHAT TO DO: Copy-edit the errors in the following sentences. There are five errors.

Our house at 220 Elm Avenue Elm Forest, Illinois, is usually the place where everybody gathers to play. Our big, beautiful back yard, is perfect for running around. My dad said, "Jimmy let's think of a game where your sisters loud voice has to be quiet!" Our brilliant, idea was to organize a game of hide and seek.

(over)

WHAT TO DO: In each sentence below there is a comma split. In the spaces below each sentence are the numbers of all the other punctuation in the sentence. Find the comma split and write its number in the space at the left. Write what it is splitting beside that comma's number below the sentence. Next to the other numbers, write the buzzword of the rule for that punctuation. Remember that each set of quotation marks counts as one thing. We will only put a number under the open quote (") mark, not the close quote (") mark.

3 1. At the start of the game,(1) my brother's(2) deep voice,(3) could be heard counting, "(4)One...two...three...!"

#1 *2+ intro prep phrases*

#2 *possessives*

#3 *splits subject and verb*

#4 *quotation marks*

3 2. My dad,(1) my sister,(2) and I all hid in different,(3) places in the yard.

#1 *items in a series*

#2 *items in a series*

#3 *splits modifier and its noun*

3 3. Well,(1) I hid behind my mom's big azalea bush,(2) but my brother gave me,(3) a big grin when he found me.

#1 *introductory single word*

#2 *compound sentence*

#3 *splits indirect object and direct object*

TEST: POSSESSIVES

NAME: ____

POINTS EARNED: ________ out of 31 ______ LEVEL: ________________

WHAT TO DO: All the sentences below contain possessives. Put the apostrophe ['] in the correct place.

__/1 1. One of my neighborhoods big traditions is to have an organized field day each spring.

__/1 2. My dads favorite event is the tug o' war.

__/2 3. The three-legged race is my favorite when my moms leg is tied to my sisters leg and they race.

__/2 4. My best friends best event is the sack race when he hops to the finish line in one of Mr. Parkers feed sacks.

__/2 5. Everybodys input is required to make our field day a success, but some folks prefer to sit in my moms lawn chairs and cheer the contestants on.

WHAT TO DO: Copy-edit the errors in the following sentences. There are five errors.

__/5 At the end of the field day we all gather together for a big hamburger and hotdog barbeque. "Jason you're in charge of everybody's drinks," said Dad. All the neighbor's bring food and the grownups talk while we kids play. My next-door neighbors potato salad is always the biggest hit.

===
13

WHAT TO DO: In each sentence below there is a comma split. In the spaces below each sentence are the numbers of all the other punctuation in the sentence. Find the comma split and write its number in the space at the left. Write what it is splitting beside that comma's number below the sentence. Next to the other numbers, write the buzzword of the rule for that punctuation. Remember that each set of quotation marks counts as one thing. We will only put a number under the open quote (") mark, not the close quote (") mark.

__2__ (—/2) 1. As a matter of fact, our, neighborhood's next field day is scheduled for Saturday, July 14, 2011.
(1 = "fact,"; 2 = "our,"; 3 = "neighborhood's"; 4 = "14,")

—/1 #1 *expressions or 2+ intro prep phrases*

—/1 #2 *splits modifier and its noun*

—/1 #3 *possessives*

—/1 #4 *names, dates, & places*

__1__ (—/2) 2. I, hope it will be a gorgeous, sunny day for the event, or we'll have to place it indoors.
(1 = "I,"; 2 = "gorgeous,"; 3 = "event,")

—/1 #1 *splits subject and verb*

—/1 #2 *two adjectives "and" test*

—/1 #3 *compound sentence*

__5__ (—/2) 3. "Jason, we need to start exercising to get ready for next year's tug o' war," Dad, said.
(1 = open quote "; 2 = "Jason,"; 3 = "year's"; 4 = "war,""; 5 = "Dad,")

—/1 #1 *quotation marks*

—/1 #2 *direct address*

—/1 #3 *possessives*

—/1 #4 *gear change comma*

—/1 #5 *splits subject and verb*

===
18

Score Range		Result
31 - 28	=	Mastery
27 - 25	=	Superiority
24 - 22	=	Competency
21 - 19	=	Probationary
18 and below	=	Repeat

CAPITALIZATION

my friend sarah goes to crabtree valley mall every sunday.

Does the sentence above look a little weird? Why? You're right! Nothing is capitalized as it should be. We use capital letters to signal our readers that a new sentence has begun or that what they're reading is the actual name of something.

You hopefully know by now that you put a capital letter at the beginning of a new sentence. You most likely capitalize your name, too, don't you? See? You're ahead of the game!

There are different reasons we capitalize, so we'll give a series of examples. The buzzword for this rule is *"capitalize."* Here are two more symbols you'll need to know for copy-editing:

change to an upper-case letter: United states
change to a lower-case letter: the blue Car

A. Capitalize the names of people and places. If a person has a title, that gets capitalized too if it comes before their name.

People: Erin, Mrs. Karl, President Reagan
Places: Italy, First Baptist Church, North Carolina, Main Street

B. Capitalize proper adjectives. When you make an adjective out of a proper noun, capitalize it.

Greek theater, Mrs. Karl's shoes, Italian meal

C. Capitalize brand names of products.

Generic Name (don't capitalize)	Brand Name (capitalize)
tissue	Kleenex
photocopier	Xerox
car	Toyota

D. Capitalize all the words in the titles of books, songs, news articles, etc., EXCEPT prepositions, articles, and conjunctions.

Gone with the Wind
Pride and Prejudice
The Adventures of Tom Sawyer
"Running the Right Way"

E. Capitalize the names of races, nationalities, and religions.

Races:	Indian, Asian, Irish-American
Nationalities:	Americans, European, Israeli
Religions:	Catholic, Buddhist, a Seventh-Day Adventist

F. Capitalize the days of the week and the months of the year.

Monday, January, March, Tuesday

CAPITALIZATION: EXERCISE #1

NAME: ____

WHAT TO DO: Circle the letters in the sentences below that need to be capitalized. Watch out for those proper adjectives; they're sneaky!

1. I just got back from a trip to smoky mountain national park.
2. it was a field trip for our sunday school class at first baptist church in richmond, virginia.
3. I shared a tent with my buddies jared, lucas, and mason.
4. our teacher mr. james greene showed us how to survive in the wild.
5. it was fun when our group met up with a bunch of guys from a catholic church group who were also camping.

WHAT TO DO: Copy-edit the errors in the following sentences. Remember, if you find a letter that needs to be capitalized, draw three shorts lines underneath it. There are **SEVEN** errors.

One of the boys in our group is of asian descent. He has never used a fishing pole in his life. Mr. greene showed Michael how to hold the pole and what to do. As soon as he put it in the water, Michaels pole dipped strongly. "Michael pull up your pole! shouted Mr. Greene. Michael was amazed when he pulled up a beautiful big fish!!

WHAT TO DO: In each sentence below there is a comma split. In the spaces below each sentence are the numbers of all the other punctuation in the sentence. Find the comma split and write its number in the space at the left. Write what it is splitting beside that comma's number below the sentence. Next to the other numbers, write the buzzword of the rule for that punctuation. Remember that each set of quotation marks counts as one thing. We will only put a number under the open quote (") mark, not the close quote (") mark.

2 1. Mr. Greene showed, Michael how to clean his fish, and we had a big, delicious fish fry for dinner.
(1 under "Mr.", 2 under "showed,", 3 under "fish,", 4 under "big,")

#1 *capitalize*

#2 *splits verb and direct object*

#3 *compound sentence*

#4 *two adjectives "and" test*

2 2. At the end of dinner, we, celebrated Michael's triumph by singing "For He's a Jolly Good Fellow."
(1 under "dinner,", 2 under "we,", 3 under "Michael's", 4 under the open quote)

#1 *2+ intro prep phrases*

#2 *splits subject and verb*

#3 *possessives*

#4 *titles*

1 3. Mr. Greene told us, some stories, and we spent the rest of the evening singing around the campfire.
(1 under "us,", 2 under "stories,")

#1 *splits indirect object and direct object*

#2 *compound sentence*

CAPITALIZATION: EXERCISE #2

NAME: ______________________________

WHAT TO DO: Circle the letters in the sentences below that need to be capitalized. Watch out for those proper adjectives; they're sneaky!

1. One day on our trip we made arrangements to camp with a a group of jewish kids from new york city.
2. Their leader was mr. jerome steinberg, and he and our mr. greene had been roommates at ohio state university.
3. we had a great time around the campfire that night as mr. greene and mr. steinberg told stories about their crazy college days.
4. Then mr. steinberg read us a scary story called "the gold bug."
5. It was a little creepy as we sat under the shadow of the great smoky mountains.

WHAT TO DO: Copy-edit the errors in the following sentences. Remember, if you find a letter that needs to be capitalized, draw three shorts lines underneath it. There are **SEVEN** errors.

At the end of the story the two leaders said "It's time to turn in guys!" We headed toward our neatly-pitched, tent and crawled into our warm sleeping bags. After a fair amount of whispering, giggling and joking, Mr. greene told us it was, time to go to sleep.

WHAT TO DO: In each sentence below there is a comma split. In the spaces below each sentence are the numbers of all the other punctuation in the sentence. Find the comma split and write its number in the space at the left. Write what it is splitting beside that comma's number below the sentence. Next to the other numbers, write the buzzword of the rule for that punctuation. Remember that each set of quotation marks counts as one thing. We will only put a number under the open quote (") mark, not the close quote (") mark.

3 1. We awoke to a cool,(1) misty morning,(2) and it was decided that we,(3) should spend the day looking for huckleberries.

#1 *two adjectives "and" test*

#2 *compound sentence*

#3 *splits subject and verb*

3 2. After all,(1) Mr.(2) Steinberg was an expert at spotting ripe, delicious,(3) huckleberries in the woods.

#1 *expressions*

#2 *capitalize*

#3 *splits modifier and its noun*

4 3. Mr. Steinberg's(1) son, Jerome Steinberg, Jr.,(2) got the most huckleberries,(3) and he got to pick out at which meal we,(4) would get to eat them!

#1 *possessives*

#2 *names, dates, & places*

#3 *compound sentence*

#4 *splits subject and verb*

CAPITALIZATION: EXERCISE #3

NAME: ______________________________

WHAT TO DO: Circle the letters in the sentences below that need to be capitalized. Watch out for those proper adjectives; they're sneaky!

1. jerome decided to use a huckleberry pancake recipe from recipes for the campfire.
2. jared, lucas, mason, and I helped him mix the pancake batter.
3. as we worked, we all sang "I've been working on the railroad" at the top of our lungs.
4. Mr. greene, mr. steinberg, and the rest of the guys declared that our creation "huckleberry morning surprise" was great.
5. We rounded out our breakfast with canadian bacon, florida orange juice, and lots of smuckers maple syrup.

WHAT TO DO: Copy-edit the errors in the following sentences. Remember, if you find a letter that needs to be capitalized, draw three shorts lines underneath it. There are **SEVEN** errors.

After our huge delicious breakfast we all pitched in to clean up our campsite. Our plan for the day was to meet up with another group of campers led by one of Mr. Greens college pals named Kent yakamoto. He had a group of boys who live in Tokyo Japan. Well we were fascinated to meet and hike with these guys!

WHAT TO DO: In each sentence below there is a comma split. In the spaces below each sentence are the numbers of all the other punctuation in the sentence. Find the comma split and write its number in the space at the left. Write what it is splitting beside that comma's number below the sentence. Next to the other numbers, write the buzzword of the rule for that punctuation. Remember that each set of quotation marks counts as one thing. We will only put a number under the open quote (") mark, not the close quote (") mark.

4 1. Well, I was paired up with a boy named Miko, and
1 2 3
this, was his first time camping.
4

#1 *introductory single word*

#2 *capitalize*

#3 *compound sentence*

#4 *splits subject and verb*

2 2. "I speak, a little English," said Miko in a soft,
1 2 3
timid voice.

#1 *quotation marks*

#2 *splits verb and direct object*

#3 *two adjectives "and" test*

2 3. Needless to say, I was, extremely relieved because
1 2
I don't speak a word of Japanese!
3

#1 *expressions*

#2 *splits linking verb and complement*

#3 *capitalize*

TEST: CAPITALIZATION

NAME: ______________________________

POINTS EARNED: ________ out of 46 ______ LEVEL: __________________

WHAT TO DO: Circle the letters in the sentences below that need to be capitalized. Watch out for those proper adjectives; they're sneaky!

__ /8 1. we baptists and our jewish and japanese hiking buddies had a great time in smoky mountain national park.

__ /5 2. Mr. greene, mr. steinberg, and mr. yakamoto kept us from getting lost on the trails.

__ /3 3. We really enjoyed our snacks of american cheese, jewish matzoh crackers, and japanese noodles.

__ /4 4. On our last night we pitched our tent a little too close to west fork creek, and I soaked my new sears sleeping bag.

__ /3 5. we decided that we should all write a book called camping for dummies!

WHAT TO DO: Copy-edit the errors in the following sentences. Remember, if you find a letter that needs to be capitalized, draw three shorts lines underneath it. There are **SEVEN** errors.

__ /7

We made, a lot of mistakes on our trip but we had a lot of fun. Our three teachers, on the other hand taught us a lot. After the loss of my sleeping bag they put together a warm dry place for me to sleep. Mr. Greenes book Hiking with Rookies was, a huge help.

=== 30

(over)

WHAT TO DO: In each sentence below there is a comma split. In the spaces below each sentence are the numbers of all the other punctuation in the sentence. Find the comma split and write its number in the space at the left. Write what it is splitting beside that comma's number below the sentence. Next to the other numbers, write the buzzword of the rule for that punctuation. Remember that each set of quotation marks counts as one thing. We will only put a number under the open quote (") mark, not the close quote (") mark.

__**3**__ / 2 1. I want to become a pen pal with Miko in Tokyo, Japan, so I got his address and put it in my little, book.

(numbers: 1 = Tokyo, 2 = Japan, 3 = little,)

__ / 1 #1 *capitalize*

__ / 1 #2 *names, dates, & places*

__ / 1 #3 *splits modifier and its noun*

__**1**__ / 2 2. My family is planning, a trip to Japan, and Miko and I are going to meet on Saturday, May 3, 2012.

(numbers: 1 = planning, 2 = Japan, 3 = Miko, 4 = Saturday,)

__ / 1 #1 *splits verb and direct object*

__ / 1 #2 *compound sentence*

__ / 1 #3 *capitalize*

__ / 1 #4 *names, dates, & places*

__**1**__ / 2 3. It will be, so much fun to visit with Miko's family and eat great Japanese food.

(numbers: 1 = be, 2 = Miko's, 3 = Japanese)

__ / 1 #1 *splits linking verb and complement*

__ / 1 #2 *possessives*

__ / 1 #3 *capitalize*

=== 16

Score Range		Result
46 - 41	=	Mastery
40 - 37	=	Superiority
36 - 32	=	Competency
31 - 28	=	Probationary
27 and below	=	Repeat

PRONOUN-ANTECEDENT AGREEMENT

Okay, it's time to think WAY back to our grammar notes. Do you remember learning about pronouns? If you've forgotten a little, now is a good time to go and review your notes on pronouns. Be sure to read over everything including what an antecedent is. It's okay ... I'll wait ...

Alright, ready?

We need to be aware of what the antecedent for a pronoun is because those two things need to agree. That means that they match in NUMBER, GENDER, and PERSON. It doesn't matter if the pronoun is doing a job (subject, direct object, etc.) or acting as a modifier. It still needs to match the antecedent.

A. NUMBER refers to whether a pronoun is singular or plural.

1. The following pronouns are singular (they refer to a single thing or person)

each	one	everybody	someone
either	anybody	everyone	nobody
neither	anyone	somebody	no one

EXAMPLES: EACH of the boys had HIS bat and ball.
EVERYONE needs to put HIS coat on.
SOMEONE had left HIS OR HER coat at church.

2. The following pronouns can be singular or plural depending on the antecedent.

all any some none

EXAMPLES: SOME of the STUDENTS looked funny in THEIR costumes.
SOME of the MILK spilled when IT was poured.

3. Two or more singular antecedents joined by OR or NOR are treated as singular.

EXAMPLES: Either Bill OR Ted will bring HIS camera.
Neither Jessica NOR Julie would repeat what SHE said.

B. GENDER refers to whether the pronoun is MASCULINE, FEMININE, or NEUTER. To put it simply -- is it a boy pronoun, a girl pronoun, or can we not tell?

EXAMPLES: The wagon lost one of ITS wheels. (neuter gender)
The waitress said HER feet were tired. (feminine gender)
The postman took HIS time. (masculine gender)

When an antecedent is meant to indicate both masculine and feminine, it is correct to use masculine pronouns. However, to be "politically correct," it is often best to use the phrase "his or her." Using "they" isn't correct. Here's an example:

SOMEONE has left THEIR books under the tree. (this is incorrect)
SOMEONE has left HIS OR HER books under the tree. (this is correct)

C. PERSON refers to the following:

I, me, my, mine, we, us, ourselves, ours, our- FIRST PERSON
you, your, yours - SECOND PERSON
he, she, him, her, his, hers, one, it, its, they, them, theirs - THIRD PERSON

EXAMPLES: (WRONG) ONE should never let YOUR sadness show.

This sentence starts off in third person and switches to second.

(RIGHT) ONE should never let ONE'S (or HIS) sadness show.

(WRONG) I find that reading in low light is hard on YOUR eyes.

This sentence starts off in first person and switches to second.

(RIGHT) I find that reading in low light is hard on MY eyes.

The buzzword for this rule is *"pronoun-antecedent agreement"* or *"pro-antec agmt."*

PRONOUN-ANTECEDENT AGREEMENT: EXERCISE #1

NAME: ______________________________

WHAT TO DO: In the sentences below circle the correct pronoun so that it agrees with its antecedent. Sentences #1 and #2 will concentrate on pronouns that agree with their antecedents in NUMBER.

1. Someone in my family needs to put (his, their) toys away.

2. Each of the toys on the family room floor belongs to (him, them).

Sentences #3 and #4 will concentrate on pronouns that agree with their antecedents in GENDER.

3. My little brother picked up his Teddy bear by (its, his, her) head.

4. I put my American Girl doll away in (its, her, his) box.

Sentences #5 and #6 will concentrate on pronouns that agree with their antecedents in PERSON.

5. One should always put away (one's, your) toys.

6. If we try hard enough, (you, we) can keep our play area neat.

WHAT TO DO: Copy-edit the errors in the following sentences. There are **SEVEN** errors.

Neither Mikey nor Lucas seems able to pick up after ~~themselves~~ himself. My mom decided to make us a list of our daily chores. I'll check off each chore you do," she said. Mikeys list wasn't very long because he is the youngest. Mom says that lucas, on the other hand needs to be reminded the most often.

(over)

WHAT TO DO: In each sentence below there is a comma split. In the spaces below each sentence are the numbers of all the other punctuation in the sentence. Find the comma split and write its number in the space at the left. Write what it is splitting beside that comma's number below the sentence. Next to the other numbers, write the buzzword of the rule for that punctuation. Remember that each set of quotation marks counts as one thing. We will only put a number under the open quote (") mark, not the close quote (") mark.

1___ 1. Mom and Dad, try to keep our house at 615 Oak
1 2
Avenue, Dayton, Ohio, as neat as possible.
3

#1 *splits subject and verb*

#2 *capitalize*

#3 *names, dates, & places*

3___ 2. "Lucas," she said, "please read, the chart which
1 2 3
lists your chores, Mikey's chores, and mine."
4

#1 *quotation marks*

#2 *gear change comma*

#3 *splits verb and direct object*

#4 *items in a series*

3___ 3. Everybody in our family needs to do his chores
1
every day, and then we have a neat, home.
2 3

#1 *pro-antec agmt*

#2 *compound sentence*

#3 *splits modifier and its noun*

PRONOUN-ANTECEDENT AGREEMENT: EXERCISE #2

NAME: ______________________________

WHAT TO DO: In the sentences below circle the correct pronoun so that it agrees with its antecedent. Sentences #1 and #2 will concentrate on pronouns that agree with their antecedents in NUMBER.

1. Each family has (its, their) own set of rules about chores.

2. Two of the families in our neighborhood changes (its, their) list each week.

Sentences #3 and #4 will concentrate on pronouns that agree with their antecedents in GENDER.

3. Sometimes it's Dad who decides what (he, she, it) wants.

4. I like it when my mom tells (you, me) what to do.

Sentences #5 and #6 will concentrate on pronouns that agree with their antecedents in PERSON.

5. A person shouldn't just tell other families what (he, they) thinks they should do.

6. Once you make a plan, however, (one, you) should stick to it.

WHAT TO DO: Copy-edit the errors in the following sentences. There are **SEVEN** errors.

Our neat beautiful house had just been cleaned. We were, ready for a visit from my uncle, Mr. Ray Johnson Jr. He is the well-known author of the book A Boys Guide to Housework. My famous uncle, firmly believes that housework is everyone's responsibility. Nobody in our house plans to forget their chores when Uncle Ray is here!

WHAT TO DO: In each sentence below there is a comma split. In the spaces below each sentence are the numbers of all the other punctuation in the sentence. Find the comma split and write its number in the space at the left. Write what it is splitting beside that comma's number below the sentence. Next to the other numbers, write the buzzword of the rule for that punctuation. Remember that each set of quotation marks counts as one thing. We will only put a number under the open quote (") mark, not the close quote (") mark.

3 1. Uncle Ray thoroughly approves of my mom's clever, chart.
(1 under "Uncle", 2 under "mom's", 3 under "clever,")

#1 *capitalize*

#2 *possessives*

#3 *splits modifier and its noun*

2 2. As a matter of fact, he has, a chapter in his book called "The Magic of Charts."
(1 under "fact,", 2 under "has,", 3 under "The Magic of Charts")

#1 *expressions*

#2 *splits verb and direct object*

#3 *titles*

2 3. Sometimes one of us forgets his chores for the day, but Uncle Ray is, a believer in making each morning a fresh, new start.
(1 under "day,", 2 under "is,", 3 under "fresh,")

#1 *compound sentence*

#2 *splits linking verb and complement*

#3 *two adjectives "and" test*

PRONOUN-ANTECEDENT AGREEMENT: EXERCISE #3

NAME: ______________________________

WHAT TO DO: In the sentences below circle the correct pronoun so that it agrees with its antecedent in NUMBER, GENDER, and PERSON.

1. Both of my brothers have (his, their) rooms to clean.
2. Only one of them is able to make (their, his) own bed.
3. "Mikey, one should always make (your, his) bed," I tell him.
4. He tries his best, but his comforter always slips out of (its, his) place.
5. Neither Mikey nor Lucas is really good at making (his, their) bed.
6. I believe that making your bed is one of (my, your) most important chores.

WHAT TO DO: Copy-edit the errors in the following sentences. There are **SEVEN** errors.

In Uncle rays book he teaches boys a song to sing to help ~~him~~ them learn to make their beds. This great little song, is called "Sheets and Pillows, Spread 'Em Up!" Putting something to music, after all, helps you remember what to do more easily. Mikey may not be able to make his bed perfectly, but he sure can sing, that song!

WHAT TO DO: In each sentence below there is a comma split. In the spaces below each sentence are the numbers of all the other punctuation in the sentence. Find the comma split and write its number in the space at the left. Write what it is splitting beside that comma's number below the sentence. Next to the other numbers, write the buzzword of the rule for that punctuation. Remember that each set of quotation marks counts as one thing. We will only put a number under the open quote (") mark, not the close quote (") mark.

3 1. "Have you ever noticed," asked Mom, " how easy it is to remember things when they are in a lively, tune?"
(1 under the opening quote, 2 under the comma after "Mom", 3 under the comma after "lively")

#1 *quotation marks*

#2 *gear change comma*

#3 *splits modifier and its noun*

2 2. "Sheets and Pillows, Spread 'Em Up" is, a great little song, and it'll result in a neat, beautiful bed.
(1 under the apostrophe in "'Em", 2 under the comma after "is", 3 under the comma after "song", 4 under the comma after "neat")

#1 *titles*

#2 *splits linking verb and complement*

#3 *compound sentence*

#4 *two adjectives "and" test*

2 3. Yes, my uncle Ray, is a firm believer in learning to make one's bed properly.
(1 under the comma after "Yes", 2 under the comma after "Ray", 3 under the apostrophe in "one's")

#1 *introductory single word*

#2 *splits subject and verb*

#3 *possessives*

TEST: PRONOUN-ANTECEDENT AGREEMENT

NAME: ______________________________

POINTS EARNED: __________ out of 28____ LEVEL: ____________________

WHAT TO DO: In the sentences below circle the correct pronoun so that it agrees with its antecedent in NUMBER, GENDER, and PERSON.

__ 1. My mom has two brothers, and each of them is an expert in (his, their) field.
1

__ 2. Each of my Uncle Bill's books has (its, their) own subject.
1

__ 3. If anybody wants to know something, (he, they) usually asks Uncle Bill.
1

__ 4. One of his books is on engine repair, and each type of engine has (his, its) own chapter.
1

__ 5. I believe that each driver should learn to keep (his, their) engine in good order.
1

__ 6. Each of my uncles has certainly made (his, their) parents proud!
1

WHAT TO DO: Copy-edit the errors in the following sentences. There are **SEVEN** errors.

My favorite of Uncle bill's books is called Training Service Dogs. This fantastic book, teaches people how to train dogs for the blind the elderly, and the disabled. There is, after all a great need for these wonderful dogs. One of his readers has trained a French poodle and he is now a service dog for a disabled man. Everyone who is disabled, should have a great companion like Rocket!

__
7

===
13

WHAT TO DO: In each sentence below there is a comma split. In the spaces below each sentence are the numbers of all the other punctuation in the sentence. Find the comma split and write its number in the space at the left. Write what it is splitting beside that comma's number below the sentence. Next to the other numbers, write the buzzword of the rule for that punctuation. Remember that each set of quotation marks counts as one thing. We will only put a number under the open quote (") mark, not the close quote (") mark.

__/2 **2** 1. "Service dogs perform, a great service, " says my uncle Bill.
1 2 3

__/1 #1 *quotation marks*

__/1 #2 *splits verb and direct object*

__/1 #3 *capitalize*

__/2 **3** 2. Each dog does its job to help the blind and the
1
disabled, and each dog becomes, a great
2 3
companion.

__/1 #1 *pro-antec agmt*

__/1 #2 *compound sentence*

__/1 #3 *splits linking verb and complement*

__/2 **3** 3. As a matter of fact, I would love to learn to train
1
these wonderful, magnificent dogs when I, grow
2 3
up.

__/1 #1 *expressions*

__/1 #2 *two adjectives "and" test*

__/1 #3 *splits subject and verb*

Score Range		**Result**
28 - 25	=	Mastery
24 - 22	=	Superiority
21 - 19	=	Competency
18 - 16	=	Probationary
16 and below	=	Repeat

===
15

SUBJECT-VERB AGREEMENT

Now we have to talk about another type of agreement. In the sentences we write, the subject and the verb need to agree. In other words, a singular subject (girl) takes a singular verb (jumps). GIRL JUMPS. A plural subject (GIRLS) takes a plural verb (JUMP). GIRLS JUMP. We usually do this naturally, our brains just know what is correct since we've been speaking for a long time. There are a few situations, though, where we need to pay attention to do it correctly.

A. When there are modifiers (especially prepositional phrases) between the subject and verb.

EXAMPLE: A **GROUP** of children **WAS** waving to the band.

GROUP is a singular noun, even though it is made up of many children. A good trick is to take out the modifiers and see what sounds right. A GROUP WAS WAVING. You wouldn't say A GROUP WERE WAVING ... that sounds funny.

B. When the subject is an indefinite pronoun. In the last unit you learned which of these pronouns are singular and which are plural. Refer to those notes again if you need to.

EXAMPLE: **EACH** of the boys **IS** a good singer.
BOTH of the boys **ARE** good singers.

Again, you can always take out the modifiers and just read the subject and verb together. You would say EACH IS and BOTH ARE. You would not say EACH ARE or BOTH IS ... that sounds funny.

C. When singular subjects are joined by OR or NOR, you use a singular verb. You're talking about one or the other, not both. That's why a singular verb is appropriate. When you join singular subjects together with AND, you use a plural verb. The subject is like an addition problem; you've added two singular things together to make a plural one!

EXAMPLE: **NEITHER** the teacher **NOR** the student **WAS** on time.
BOTH the teacher **AND** the student **ARE** on time.

The "buzzword" for this rule is *subj-verb agmt.*

SUBJECT-VERB AGREEMENT: EXERCISE #1

NAME: ______________________________

WHAT TO DO: In the sentences below circle the correct verb so that it agrees with its subject.

1. Each of the families in my Sunday School group (is, are) planning what they want to do for Thanksgiving.
2. Two of the groups (is, are) traveling to visit their grandparents.
3. Neither of those two families (is, are) traveling very far, though.
4. Last year a bunch of the kids (was, were) just staying at home.
5. But this year nobody in all the classes (is, are) staying at home.

WHAT TO DO: Copy-edit the errors in the following sentences. There are **SEVEN** errors.

Neither my mom nor my dad were very excited about staying home last year. "To be honest, said my mom, "it's just a lot of work for our whole family!" She said she'd be more than, happy to let someone else do the cooking this year! As a matter of fact I really enjoy playing with my cousins' toys at their house! Of course, we always bring, a special side dish to help out with dinner. I just love the turkey, stuffing, mashed potatoes and cranberry sauce. I can almost smell the delicious tempting aroma of pumpkin pie!

WHAT TO DO: In each sentence below there is a comma split. In the spaces below each sentence are the numbers of all the other punctuation in the sentence. Find the comma split and write its number in the space at the left. Write what it is splitting beside that comma's number below the sentence. Next to the other numbers, write the buzzword of the rule for that punctuation. Remember that each set of quotation marks counts as one thing. We will only put a number under the open quote (") mark, not the close quote (") mark.

2 1. At the beginning of Thanksgiving dinner,(1) everybody,(2) always says what he's thankful for.(3)

#1 *2+ intro prep phrases*

#2 *splits subject and verb*

#3 *subject verb agreement*

4 2. "(1)I'm thankful for my family, my friends,(2) and my dog Coco,(3)" said my little,(4) cousin Samantha.

#1 *quotations*

#2 *items in a series*

#3 *gear change comma*

#4 *splits modifier and its noun*

1 3. It is also,(1) a custom for our family to sing "Bless This House,(2)" and we've(3) gotten pretty good at it!

#1 *splits linking verb and complement*

#2 *titles*

#3 *gear change comma or compound sentence*

SUBJECT-VERB AGREEMENT: EXERCISE #2

NAME: ______________________________

WHAT TO DO: In the sentences below circle the correct verb so that it agrees with its subject.

1. Unfortunately, neither my dad nor my brother (sings, sing) very well.
2. So each of the other family members (tries, try) to sing really loudly to drown them out.
3. After the song, everybody in our family (pitches, pitch) in to clean up.
4. Neither my little niece nor my baby brother (is, are) to be trusted with clearing the table.
5. One of my family members (is, are) always in charge of handling the china.

WHAT TO DO: Copy-edit the errors in the following sentences. There are **SEVEN** errors.

This year Thanksgiving is on Thursday November 26, which is also my dads birthday! So everybody else in the family, decided to make an extra big pumpkin pie with "Happy Birthday" written on it. Then, after we sang "Bless This House," we all sang the song Happy Birthday. As a matter of fact Dad was pretty pleased with our surprise birthday pie. He gave my mom, a big kiss and said, "Thanks, Honey!

WHAT TO DO: In each sentence below there is a comma split. In the spaces below each sentence are the numbers of all the other punctuation in the sentence. Find the comma split and write its number in the space at the left. Write what it is splitting beside that comma's number below the sentence. Next to the other numbers, write the buzzword of the rule for that punctuation. Remember that each set of quotation marks counts as one thing. We will only put a number under the open quote (") mark, not the close quote (") mark.

2 1. Yes,(1) we have several Thanksgiving,(2) traditions in our family,(3) but my favorite one involves my uncles.

#1 *introductory single word*

#2 *splits modifier and its noun*

#3 *compound sentence*

1 2. Each uncle sits everyone down and tells us,(1) an outrageous,(2) elaborate story about his younger days.(3)

#1 *splits indirect object and direct object*

#2 *two adjectives "and" test*

#3 *pro-antec agmt*

2 3. Uncle Joe's(1) stories are usually,(2) completely untrue,(3) as a matter of fact.

#1 *possessives*

#2 *splits linking verb and complement*

#3 *expressions*

SUBJECT-VERB AGREEMENT: EXERCISE #3

NAME: ____

WHAT TO DO: In the sentences below circle the correct verb so that it agrees with its subject.

1. All of my uncles (tries, try) to outdo each other with their stories.
2. Neither Uncle Bill nor Uncle Jay (is, are) able to top Uncle Joe's stories.
3. Each of them (try, tries) really hard every year, but usually Uncle Joe wins.
4. A small group of us children (votes, vote) on whose story is best.
5. This year nobody (was, were) hesitant; the winner was Uncle Joe again!

WHAT TO DO: Copy-edit the errors in the following sentences. There are **SEVEN** errors.

This year Uncle Joes story was called The Night They Burned the Outhouse. He swears this story took place on October 31 1975, in the town where he grew up. The story, involves his best friend his high school football coach, and an old outhouse. No one in our family actually believe Uncle Joe, but we sure have, a great time listening to him!

WHAT TO DO: In each sentence below there is a comma split. In the spaces below each sentence are the numbers of all the other punctuation in the sentence. Find the comma split and write its number in the space at the left. Write what it is splitting beside that comma's number below the sentence. Next to the other numbers, write the buzzword of the rule for that punctuation. Remember that each set of quotation marks counts as one thing. We will only put a number under the open quote (") mark, not the close quote (") mark.

2 1. Uncle Jay's story this year was called, "Old Mrs.
1 2 3
Sherwood's Grey Sweater."

#1 *possessives*

#2 *splits verb and direct object*

#3 *titles*

3 2. Yes, it's about one of his teachers from Elmwood
1 2
Elementary School who had, this ratty old grey
3
sweater.

#1 *introductory single word*

#2 *capitalize*

#3 *splits verb and direct object*

3 3. He swears that there was a fire in Mrs. Sherwood's

classroom, but that neither he nor his best friend
1
was, responsible.
2 3

#1 *compound sentence*

#2 *subj-verb agmt*

#3 *splits linking verb and complement*

TEST: SUBJECT-VERB AGREEMENT

NAME: ______________________________

POINTS EARNED: ________ out of 28 ________ LEVEL: ______________

WHAT TO DO: In the sentences below circle the correct verb so that it agrees with its subject.

__ 1. Both my uncle Jay and my uncle Joe (remember, remembers) Uncle Bill's story.
1

__ 2. Once an old pair of Uncle Bill's jeans (was, were) eaten by a cow!
1

__ 3. Each of my uncles (swear, swears) that this is a true story.
1

__ 4. Either Uncle Bill or Uncle Joe (was, were) present when the cow ate the pants.
1

__ 5. It happened when a herd of cows (was, were) quietly grazing in a meadow one hot summer day.
1

WHAT TO DO: Copy-edit the errors in the following sentences. There are **SEVEN** errors.

According to Uncle Bills story, he and one of his brothers set out for a walk on a hot steamy summer day. Uncle Bill was wearing his favorite pair of jeans which had not been washed for weeks!He got so hot he decided to take his jeans off and hung them on the meadow fence. One curious cow came over and started to sniff Uncle Bill's jeans. The dirty, sweaty jeans must have smelled interesting to the cow because she started to eat them! "Let go of my jeans! yelled Uncle Bill. This is how we learned the story The Day the Cow Ate My Jeans by my uncle Bill.

__
7

===
12

WHAT TO DO: In each sentence below there is a comma split. In the spaces below each sentence are the numbers of all the other punctuation in the sentence. Find the comma split and write its number in the space at the left. Write what it is splitting beside that comma's number below the sentence. Next to the other numbers, write the buzzword of the rule for that punctuation. Remember that each set of quotation marks counts as one thing. We will only put a number under the open quote (") mark, not the close quote (") mark.

2 __ / 2

1. Needless to say, the whole family loves to hear my
   1
   uncles' stories after Thanksgiving, dinner, but each year
   2 3
   they have to work harder to outdo each other.

__ / 1 #1 *expressions*

__ / 1 #2 *splits modifier and its noun*

__ / 1 #3 *compound sentence*

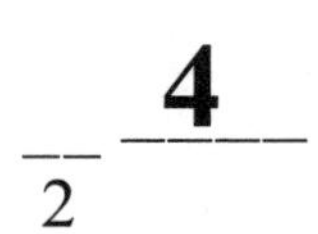

4 __ / 2

2. After the vote from all the kids, we declared Uncle
   1
   Joe the winner of this year's story-telling, contest.
   2 3 4

__ / 1 #1 *2+ intro prep phrases*

__ / 1 #2 *capitalize*

__ / 1 #3 *possessives*

__ / 1 #4 *splits modifier and its noun*

3 __ / 2

3. "Just wait until next year," said Uncle Jay, "and
   1 2
   I'll beat, you yet!"
   3

__ / 1 #1 *quotation marks*

__ / 1 #2 *gear change comma*

__ / 1 #3 *splits verb and direct object*

=== / 16

Score Range		Result
28 - 25	=	Mastery
24 - 22	=	Superiority
21 - 20	=	Competency
19 - 17	=	Probationary
16 and below	=	Repeat

WHICH PRONOUN?

Only three more units to go! Take a moment to look back at all you've learned so far. Good for you!

Now take a moment to look back at your Jr. Analytical Grammar book, Unit #3 Notes. See how the lists of pronouns are divided into columns? The columns are labeled Objective, Nominative, etc. Every wonder why? Well, here's where your question is answered!

Do these sentences sounds funny?

Me went to the store.
Marie went with I to the store.

How would you say them correctly?

I went to the store.
Marie went with me to the store.

Hmmm ... both I and ME mean the same thing, don't they? Then why the difference? Well, if you take a moment to diagram those sentences, you'll see that the pronoun in each sentence is doing a different job. In the first sentence, it's the subject. In the second sentence it's the object of the preposition.

The **nominative** case is used for subjects and predicate nominatives.

The **objective** case is used for direct objects, indirect objects, and objects of the preposition.

Nominative pronouns: I, we, you, he, she, it, they, who, whoever
Objective pronouns: me, us, you, him, her, it, them, whom, whomever

So why do you need to know all this "nominative" and "objective" stuff? I mean, you can tell what "sounds right," can't you? You're right about that, but we will discuss later why you need to know the "case" of your pronoun. Now that we've covered that, here are a few other rules to know:

A. When you use the personal pronouns I or ME along with another noun, always PUT THE OTHER GUY FIRST.

Example: (wrong) He told me and Jeff to come back later.
(correct) He told Jeff and me to come back later.

B. When listing multiple people, place them in the appropriate "social" order. That means LADIES BEFORE GENTLEMEN and OLDER FOLKS BEFORE YOUNGER.

Example: (wrong) My dad, my mom, my grandpa, and I went to the mall.
(correct) My grandpa, my mom, my dad, and I went to the mall.

C. Do you say, "Give the package to Bob or I," or "Give the package to Bob or me"? What about, "Tommy and she had a great time," or "Tommy and her had a great time"? Sometimes it's hard to tell, but I have a trick! It's called TAKE THE OTHER GUY OUT.

Let's take a look at the first one. If you take out "Bob or," you're left with:

Give the package to I.
or
Give the package to me.

Now try taking "Tommy and" out of the second sentence.

She had a great time.
or
Her had a great time.

You can tell which way "sounds right," can't you? This "take the other guy out" trick works well most of the time. When it doesn't, you can always go back to the grammar you know. Remember all that nominative case and objective case stuff we talked about? Well, let's look at these two sentences from the grammar angle. We'll figure it out without using our TAKE THE OTHER GUY OUT trick.

Give the package to Bob or me.

In this sentence, what job is "me" doing? It's the object of the preposition (to Bob or me), right? So, we need the objective case. "Me" is the objective case personal pronoun; that's why it works!

Tommy and she had a great time.

What job is "she" doing? It's the subject of the sentence (along with Tommy … it's a compound subject). Subjects need the nominative case; that's why "she" sounds right in that sentence.

The buzzword for this is *"which pronoun."*

WHICH PRONOUN?: EXERCISE #1

NAME: ____

WHAT TO DO: In the sentences below circle the correct word or group of words.

1. (Me and my brother/My brother and I) decided to have a reading contest.
2. (Him and me/He and I) love to read adventure and mystery stories.
3. Every week (my mom, my brother, and I/my brother, my mom, and I) go to the library.
4. We always ask the librarian to save the good new books for (Bob and I/ Bob and me.)
5. Mom always challenges (Bob and me/ me and Bob) to see who can read the most pages each day.

WHAT TO DO: Copy-edit the errors in the following sentences. There are **SEVEN** errors.

My brother and I have recently discovered the Hardy Boys series of books. Yes, these are old books, but they're really fun to read. My cousins Reagan and Molly love the Nancy Drew series, which became popular about the same time as the Hardy Boys. In the Nancy Drew books Nancy, Bess, and George are best friends who solve all sorts of mysteries. In the case of the Hardy Boys, the two Hardy brothers, Frank and Joe, also stumble upon and solve mysteries of all kinds.

WHAT TO DO: In each sentence below there is a comma split. In the spaces below each sentence are the numbers of all the other punctuation in the sentence. Find the comma split and write its number in the space at the left. Write what it is splitting beside that comma's number below the sentence. Next to the other numbers, write the buzzword of the rule for that punctuation. Remember that each set of quotation marks counts as one thing. We will only put a number under the open quote (") mark, not the close quote (") mark.

2 1. When my brother and I, go to the library, there are so
1 2
many Hardy Boys books to choose from!
3

#1 *which pronoun?*

#2 *splits subject and verb*

#3 *capitalize*

3 2. As a matter of fact, Hardy Boys book have been
1
written since 1927, and they are still, popular.
2 3

#1 *expressions*

#2 *compound sentence*

#3 *splits linking verb and complement*

2 3. These exciting, adventurous stories are now called,
1 2
Undercover Brothers.
3

#1 *two adjectives "and" test*

#2 *splits verb and direct object*

#3 *titles*

WHICH PRONOUN?: EXERCISE #2

NAME: ____

WHAT TO DO: In the sentences below circle the correct word or group of words.

1. Finally my mom said that (my brother and me/ my brother and I) had to stop reading Hardy Boys mysteries and try different kinds of books.

2. The librarian knows what we like, so she saves all the good new books for (Jason and me/ me and Jason).

3. Reagan and Molly use the same library, and (she and Molly/ her and Molly) think we have the best librarian in the world!

4. (Reagan, Molly, and Aunt Ruth/ Aunt Ruth, Reagan, and Molly) try to visit the library once a week at the same time we go.

5. After we get our new books (their family and us/ their family and we) all go to lunch together.

WHAT TO DO: Copy-edit the errors in the following sentences. There are **SEVEN** errors.

Molly says her first Nancy drew book was, The Secret in the Old Clock. She got it from her Uncle Bill for her birthday on April 18 2009. She says she didn't think it would be that interesting but she couldn't put it down once she started. "To tell you the truth, she said, "I ended up reading it under the covers with my dads flashlight!"

WHAT TO DO: In each sentence below there is a comma split. In the spaces below each sentence are the numbers of all the other punctuation in the sentence. Find the comma split and write its number in the space at the left. Write what it is splitting beside that comma's number below the sentence. Next to the other numbers, write the buzzword of the rule for that punctuation. Remember that each set of quotation marks counts as one thing. We will only put a number under the open quote (") mark, not the close quote (") mark.

1 1. Molly, tells of a time when she had the flu, and her Uncle Bill bought her four new Nancy Drews!
(1: comma after "Molly"; 2: comma after "flu"; 3: capital U in "Uncle")

#1 *splits subject and verb*

#2 *compound sentence*

#3 *capitalize*

3 2. Each of her uncles got her what he thought she'd like, but Uncle Bill's gift was, her very favorite.
(1: "he"; 2: apostrophe in "Bill's"; 3: comma after "was")

#1 *pro-antec agmt*

#2 *possessives*

#3 *splits linking verb and complement*

3 3. While she was getting her strength back, Molly relaxed and read her wonderful, exciting, books.
(1: capital M in "Molly"; 2: comma after "wonderful"; 3: comma after "exciting")

#1 *capitalize*

#2 *two adjectives "and" test*

#3 *splits modifier and its noun*

WHICH PRONOUN?: EXERCISE #3

NAME: ______________________________

WHAT TO DO: In the sentences below circle the correct word or group of words.

1. (My brother and I/Me and my brother) also love to read books about true adventures.

2. (He and I/Him and me) just finished one about a man who trekked through the jungles of the Amazon.

3. (Him/He) and his hiking partners met met different tribal people who live in the Amazonian jungle.

4. (They/Them) and the tribal people were very curious about each other.

5. He kepts a journal for (him/he) and his family to read after he got home.

WHAT TO DO: Copy-edit the errors in the following sentences. There are **SEVEN** errors.

I
Me and jason decided that we were going to go on an adventure when we grow up. To tell you the truth we haven't decided where we'll go yet but we sure plan to do it. Then we'll write a book called Two Brothers' Adventures and become famous! Jasons first choice is to climb Mount Everest, but neither of us is are sure where we'll really go.

WHAT TO DO: In each sentence below there is a comma split. In the spaces below each sentence are the numbers of all the other punctuation in the sentence. Find the comma split and write its number in the space at the left. Write what it is splitting beside that comma's number below the sentence. Next to the other numbers, write the buzzword of the rule for that punctuation. Remember that each set of quotation marks counts as one thing. We will only put a number under the open quote (") mark, not the close quote (") mark.

1 1. My cousins, (1) also have plans to do something totally, (2) absolutely wonderful, (3) but they haven't decided what yet.

#1 *splits subject and verb*

#2 *two adjectives "and" test*

#3 *compound sentence*

2 2. Well, (1) they can't decide if they want to be, (2) teachers, social workers, (3) or doctors.

#1 *introductory single word*

#2 *splits linking verb and complement*

#3 *items in a series*

3 3. Reagan's (1) first choice is medicine, (2) and she's already written her doctor, (3) a letter asking for advice.

#1 *possessives*

#2 *compound sentence*

#3 *splits indirect object and direct object*

TEST: WHICH PRONOUN?

NAME: ______________________________

POINTS EARNED: ________ out of 27 ______ LEVEL: ____________________

WHAT TO DO: In the sentences below circle the correct word or group of words.

__ 1 1. (Reagan, Molly, Jason, and I/ Jason, Reagan, Molly, and I) all love to read books of all kinds.

__ 1 2. (Us/We) and our moms are well known at the local library.

__ 1 3. Every book we read teaches (us/we) and our cousins something new.

__ 1 4. Our teacher told (Jason and I/Jason and me) that reading books would increase our vocabularies.

__ 1 5. (Me and Jason/Jason and I) should have the biggest vocabularies in town with all the reading we do!

WHAT TO DO: Copy-edit the errors in the following sentences. There are **SEVEN** errors.

Everybody in my bunch of friends loves to read. The best conversation-starter at our lunch table is, "Guess what I'm reading!" After the description of the book, we all usually want to read the same book. Our latest craze has been The Chronicles of Narnia. Our teacher, Miss mitchell, thinks it's pretty funny when we complain about book reports. "Jason, you give a book report at lunch every day!" she said.

__ 7

=== 12

WHAT TO DO: In each sentence below there is a comma split. In the spaces below each sentence are the numbers of all the other punctuation in the sentence. Find the comma split and write its number in the space at the left. Write what it is splitting beside that comma's number below the sentence. Next to the other numbers, write the buzzword of the rule for that punctuation. Remember that each set of quotation marks counts as one thing. We will only put a number under the open quote (") mark, not the close quote (") mark.

__/2 **3** 1. Miss Mitchell asked us one day,(1) "What's(2) going on in your head when you're reading,(3) a really good book?"

__/1 #1 *capitalize*

__/1 #2 *gear change comma*

__/1 #3 *splits verb and direct object*

__/2 **3** 2. To be honest,(1) we just stared at her at first,(2) but then Michael,(3) slowly raised his hand.

__/1 #1 *expressions*

__/1 #2 *compound sentence*

__/1 #3 *splits subject and verb*

__/2 **2** 3. "Miss Mitchell,(1) last night when I was reading,(2) *The Silver Chair*,(3) I had a whole movie going in my head," he said.

__/1 #1 *direct address*

__/1 #2 *splits verb and direct object*

__/1 #3 *titles*

Score Range		Result
27 - 24	=	Mastery
23 - 22	=	Superiority
21 - 19	=	Competency
18 - 16	=	Probationary
15 and below	=	Repeat

===
15

ADJECTIVE OR ADVERB

It's time to think back to all that grammar you learned before in Jr. Analtyical Grammar. Do you remember the difference between an adjective and an adverb? If you're a little rusty, now is a good time to go over those notes again. Go ahead; we'll wait!

Okay, ready? Sometimes people use an adjective when they should use an adverb. It's a common grammatical error. Here is an example:

(incorrect) That jacket fits her perfect.
(correct) That jacket fits her perfectly.

We need to use the adverb "perfectly" to describe HOW the jacket fits. You should never use an adjective to do an adverb's job.

The most trouble seems to come from the difference between the adjectives GOOD and BAD and the adverbs WELL and BADLY.

A. GOOD and BAD are adjectives that either modify nouns or act as predicate adjectives.

EXAMPLE: It was a GOOD day for a shopping trip.

B. WELL and BADLY are adverbs that modify verbs or other modifiers.

EXAMPLE: He did WELL on the test.

C. WELL is used as an adjective ONLY when it means "in good health."

EXAMPLE: I haven't felt WELL in days.

When using comparatives and superlatives, be sure you are using the correct form. Not all the time, but usually adjectives get "-er" or "-est" on the end. Adverbs have "more" or "most" added in front.

WORD	COMPARATIVE	SUPERLATIVE
(adj) quiet	quieter	quietest
(adv) quietly	more quietly	most quietly

(wrong) This machine will run quieter than the other.
(correct) This machine will run more quietly than the other.

The "buzzword" for this rule is *adjective or adverb.*

ADJECTIVE OR ADVERB: EXERCISE #1

NAME: ______________________________

WHAT TO DO: Circle the correct word in the sentences below.

1. Jason's mom decided that his Sunday clothes didn't fit (good/well) any more.

2. Just six months ago they had fit (perfect/perfectly)!

3. Jason just didn't feel (good/well) about wearing those short pants to church.

4. He felt (bad/badly) that his parents had to spend more money on him so soon.

5. His dad said he was just growing so (quick/quickly) that there was no help for it!

WHAT TO DO: Copy-edit the errors in the following sentences. There are **SEVEN** errors.

"We need to buy you some new sunday pants, said Mom. "You'll also need a couple of new dress shirts." The sweater Jason had been wearing to church still fit good. Jasons mom decided that the next day would be a good day to go shopping but then she remembered that Jason had a dentist appointment. To tell you the truth Jason would rather have gone shopping than go to the dentist. He really wasn't afraid of kind gentle Dr. Mason, but he hated having to keep his mouth open so long!

WHAT TO DO: In each sentence below there is a comma split. In the spaces below each sentence are the numbers of all the other punctuation in the sentence. Find the comma split and write its number in the space at the left. Write what it is splitting beside that comma's number below the sentence. Next to the other numbers, write the buzzword of the rule for that punctuation. Remember that each set of quotation marks counts as one thing. We will only put a number under the open quote (") mark, not the close quote (") mark.

2___ 1. At the dentist's office Jason read his book while he waited for his, appointment with Dr. Mason.
(numbers: 1 under "dentist's", 2 under "his,", 3 under "Dr.")

#1 *possessives*

#2 *splits modifier and its noun*

#3 *capitalize*

3___ 2. "Let's see how things look, Jason," Dr. Mason, said.
(numbers: 1 under the opening quote, 2 under "Jason,", 3 under "Mason,")

#1 *quotation marks*

#2 *direct address*

#3 *splits subject and verb*

2___ 3. At the end of his appointment, Jason was, proud to announce that his teeth looked perfect.
(numbers: 1 under "appointment,", 2 under "was,", 3 under "perfect.")

#1 *2+ intro prep phrases*

#2 *splits linking verb and complement*

#3 *adjective or adverb*

ADJECTIVE OR ADVERB: EXERCISE #2

NAME: ____

WHAT TO DO: Circle the correct word in the sentences below.

1. The next morning Jason said, "Mom, I don't feel very (good/well).

2. Mom took his temperature and said, "This doesn't look (good/well).

3. Jason began to cough (more often/oftener) than he usually did.

4. "It would be (good/well) for you to stay at home today," said Mom.

5. So Jason would have to wait (patient/patiently) for his new Sunday clothes.

WHAT TO DO: Copy-edit the errors in the following sentences. There are **SEVEN** errors.

After a few days of rest Jason felt better and Mom decided that they could go shopping for his new shirts and pants. Jason always felt he needed a book called Shopping for Dummies, but Mom knew exactly where to go. She headed for the best store in Elmwood Ohio. "May I help you Ma'am?" asked the clerk in the store. He showed Jason two different styles of pants, but neither of them were what he wanted. Jason finally, chose a navy pair of pants, a yellow shirt, and a pale blue shirt.

WHAT TO DO: In each sentence below there is a comma split. In the spaces below each sentence are the numbers of all the other punctuation in the sentence. Find the comma split and write its number in the space at the left. Write what it is splitting beside that comma's number below the sentence. Next to the other numbers, write the buzzword of the rule for that punctuation. Remember that each set of quotation marks counts as one thing. We will only put a number under the open quote (") mark, not the close quote (") mark.

1 1. Jason really liked, the way his new shirts fit smoothly
1 2
around the arms, and his pants were very comfortable.
3

#1 *splits verb and direct object*

#2 *adjective or adverb*

#3 *compound sentence*

1 2. All his new, clothes went perfectly with his older
1 2
brother's cream-colored sweater.
3

#1 *splits modifier and its noun*

#2 *adjective or adverb*

#3 *possessives*

3 3. "Yes, you can have my old sweater," said his
1 2
brother. "I've decided to start wearing, a jacket
3
to church like Dad does."

#1 *quotation marks*

#2 *introductory single word*

#3 *splits verb and direct object*

ADJECTIVE OR ADVERB: EXERCISE #3

NAME: ______________________________

WHAT TO DO: Circle the correct word in the sentences below.

1. On the next Sunday Jason thought he looked (good/well) in his new clothes.

2. The sun shone (bright/brightly) on the family as they walked into church.

3. Since they were a bit late, they walked (quicker/more quickly) than usual to their seats.

4. Jason felt (bad/badly) for all the boys in church who were wearing old clothes.

5. Then he realized that he should be thinking more (appropriate/appropriately) in church!

WHAT TO DO: Copy-edit the errors in the following sentences. There are **SEVEN** errors.

After church the family greeted Pastor newell as they left the building. "How are you Jason?" he asked. "I was sick last week, but now I'm good," Jason replied. Pastor Newell noticed Jason's new clothes and said he was looking, very handsome in them. "I have new pants, two new shirts and a new sweater!" said Jason. "Between you and I," said the pastor, "you have, very good taste!"

WHAT TO DO: In each sentence below there is a comma split. In the spaces below each sentence are the numbers of all the other punctuation in the sentence. Find the comma split and write its number in the space at the left. Write what it is splitting beside that comma's number below the sentence. Next to the other numbers, write the buzzword of the rule for that punctuation. Remember that each set of quotation marks counts as one thing. We will only put a number under the open quote (") mark, not the close quote (") mark.

1 1. Jason was very,[1] pleased to have his new clothes praised by his church's[2] pastor,[3] but he didn't want to look too proud.

#1 *splits linking verb and complement*

#2 *possessives*

#3 *compound sentence*

3 2. "Well,[1] my mom helped me pick them out," he said,[2] "and she has,[3] really good taste."

#1 *introductory single word*

#2 *gear change comma*

#3 *splits verb and direct object*

3 3. Pastor Newell smiled, winked at Jason,[1] and said,[2] "To tell you the truth, Mrs. Newell picks out most of my,[3] clothes too!"

#1 *items in a series*

#2 *expressions*

#3 *splits modifier and its noun*

TEST: ADJECTIVE OR ADVERB

NAME: ______________________________

POINTS EARNED: ________ out of 27 ____ LEVEL: ____________________

WHAT TO DO: Circle the correct word in the sentences below.

__/1 1. On the way home from church, Dad drove the car (slow/slowly).

__/1 2. Jason and his brother were traveling (quieter/more quietly) than usual.

__/1 3. "Are you feeling (good/well), boys?" asked Dad.

__/1 4. "I think I spoke too (proud/proudly) about my new clothes," said Jason.

__/1 5. "That's okay," said his brother, "most people feel (good/well) about themselves when they have new clothes."

WHAT TO DO: Copy-edit the errors in the following sentences. There are **SEVEN** errors.

__/7

"I distinctly, remember a time when I was wearing a new pair of shoes," said Mom. "My mother and ~~me~~ I were in a store and I spotted a friend of mine from school. My mother, told me there was no need to mention my new shoes. I gave my mother, a look because I didn't understand why I shouldn't mention my shoes. On the other hand I didn't want to disobey her. As soon as I saw my friends eyes looking at my shoes, however, I couldn't resist saying that they were new!"

===/12

WHAT TO DO: In each sentence below there is a comma split. In the spaces below each sentence are the numbers of all the other punctuation in the sentence. Find the comma split and write its number in the space at the left. Write what it is splitting beside that comma's number below the sentence. Next to the other numbers, write the buzzword of the rule for that punctuation. Remember that each set of quotation marks counts as one thing. We will only put a number under the open quote (") mark, not the close quote (") mark.

__**2**__ / 2 1. "Look at my new shoes!" I said. "I just bought, them
1 2
at Leonard's department store!"
3

__ / 1 #1 *quotation marks*

__ / 1 #2 *splits verb and direct object*

__ / 1 #3 *capitalize*

__**2**__ / 2 2. "Margaret, what did I tell you?" asked my, mother.
1 2
"Why, you deliberately disobeyed me!"
3

__ / 1 #1 *direct address*

__ / 1 #2 *splits modifier and its noun*

__ / 1 #3 *introductory single word*

__**1**__ / 2 3. I was terribly, sorry that I had bragged about my
1
shoes, but I had been unable to resist the look of
2
interest on my friend's face.
3

__ / 1 #1 *splits linking verb and complement*

__ / 1 #2 *compound sentence*

__ / 1 #3 *possessives*

=== / 15

Score Range		Result
27 - 24	=	Mastery
23 - 22	=	Superiority
21 - 19	=	Competency
18 - 16	=	Probationary
15 and below	=	Repeat

TRANSITIVE AND INTRANSITIVE VERBS

Oh my goodness! Just pause here for a moment and think about how much you've learned already. Now, take a moment, stand up, and do a silly dance to celebrate reaching the LAST UNIT OF THE BOOK! ***Woo hoo!!!!!***

Okay, sit down again and let's finish this thing!

A. Transitive verbs are verbs which can take a direct object. In other words, they "**transport**" (can you imagine a truck delivering something) the action of the subject to the direct object.

(I'm transporting a delivery!)

SUBJECT -------->TRANSITIVE VERB ------> DIRECT OBJECT

HAVE is a transitive verb. It has to be paired with a direct object:

I *have* lunch. I *have* a book. I *have* a sleepover next week.

Try using HAVE without a direct object. I HAVE. Huh? That doesn't work!

B. Intransitive verbs never take a direct object. Try the verb ARRIVE. You can't have a direct object with that verb. I ARRIVE ______. Nope. You don't ever ARRIVE anything; you just ARRIVE.

C. Many verbs can be transitive in some sentences and intransitive in others. Look at the following two sentences that both use the verb EATS:

He eats lunch.	He eats quickly.
(transitive)	*(intransitive)*

D. There are a few common verbs we use that change depending on whether you want the transitive or the intransitive version. We're going to talk about three VERY common sets in this unit. They are ***lay/lie, sit/set,*** and ***raise/rise***.

	PRESENT TENSE	PAST TENSE
transitive-------->	lay(s)	laid
intransitive------>	lie(s)	lay(s)

The chicken ***lays*** the egg.
They ***lie*** on the grass.

The chicken ***laid*** the egg yesterday.
They ***lay*** on the grass yesterday.

	PRESENT TENSE	PAST TENSE
transitive-------->	raise(s)	raised
intransitive------>	rise(s)	rose

They ***raise*** the flag.	They ***raised*** the flag yesterday.
The sun ***rises***.	The sun ***rose*** yesterday.

	PRESENT TENSE	PAST TENSE
transitive-------->	set(s)	set
intransitive------>	sit	sat

She ***set*** the book down.	She ***set*** the book down yesterday.
They ***sit*** down.	They ***sat*** down yesterday.

Here is one way to remember the difference. The intransitive verbs are all things you can do as an action with your own body. You lie down, you rise up, you sit down ... right? The transitive verbs are all things you do to something else. You set a book down, you raise a flag, you lay an egg. The hard part is just keeping them straight in your head.

Feel free to take a little time to make a cheat sheet for these terms. Maybe drawing pictures of the actions will help you keep them straight. Remember, these notes are here for you to use all the time. Use them! Good luck!

The buzzword for this rule is *"transitive/intransitive verbs."*

TRANSITIVE & INTRANSITIVE VERBS: EXERCISE #1

NAME: ______________________________

WHAT TO DO: Circle the correct word in the sentences below.

1. I always love to talk to Grandma about her childhood on the farm as she (sits/sets) on the porch.

2. Even before the sun (raised/rose) she and her brothers were up to do their chores.

3. One of her jobs was to pick up the hens' eggs every morning and carefully (lay/lie) them in her basket.

4. Her father had 12 hens contentedly (sitting/setting) on their nests.

5. Some days the hens would (lie/lay) one egg each!

WHAT TO DO: Copy-edit the errors in the following sentences. There are **SEVEN** errors.

"After I picked up the eggs, said Grandma, "I'd take them into the house so Ma could make breakfast. We took what we needed for breakfast and anything left over would be taken to Mr. Taylors store in the town to sell. As a matter of fact it was my job to take the eggs into town to Mr. taylor every day. Ma and I would use our egg money to buy dress fabric, curtain material and other things that our feminine hearts craved. Yes I have many good memories about Ma and me and that egg money!"

WHAT TO DO: In each sentence below there is a comma split. In the spaces below each sentence are the numbers of all the other punctuation in the sentence. Find the comma split and write its number in the space at the left. Write what it is splitting beside that comma's number below the sentence. Next to the other numbers, write the buzzword of the rule for that punctuation. Remember that each set of quotation marks counts as one thing. We will only put a number under the open quote (") mark, not the close quote (") mark.

1 1. My great-grandfather was,(1) a sergeant in the United(2) States Marine Corps during World War II,(3) and he had a flagpole in the yard.

#1 *splits linking verb and complement*

#2 *capitalize*

#3 *compound sentence*

2 2. My great-uncle Tom's(1) job,(2) was to raise the flag and play "(3)America the Beautiful" on his bugle!

#1 *possessives*

#2 *splits subject and verb*

#3 *titles*

2 3. Everybody in the family knew his(1) job and did it every,(2) morning in this busy,(3) energetic family.

#1 *pro-antec agmt*

#2 *splits modifier and its noun*

#3 *two adjectives "and" test*

TRANSITIVE & INTRANSITIVE VERBS: EXERCISE #2

NAME: ____

WHAT TO DO: Circle the correct word in the sentences below.

1. One of Grandma's jobs was to (sit/set) the table before meals.
2. She would carefully (lie/lay) the forks, knives, and spoons at each place.
3. Her mother was determined to (rise/raise) her children with good table manners.
4. After the family (sat/set) down at the table, they would say grace.
5. After lunch her mother would (lie/lay) down for a rest while Grandma did the dishes.

WHAT TO DO: Copy-edit the errors in the following sentences. There are **SEVEN** errors.

Grandma has two brothers named tom and Edward. Tom is the eldest of all three children, and he took over the farm after his father, passed away. He was an expert on farm management, and he wrote a book on it called Anybody Can Manage a Farm. Uncle Toms book was published on June 3 1967, and the whole family was, extremely proud. I once visited Uncle Tom on the farm, and I noticed that he always maintained his equipment perfect!. He said that was one of the most important things about being a successful farmer.

WHAT TO DO: In each sentence below there is a comma split. In the spaces below each sentence are the numbers of all the other punctuation in the sentence. Find the comma split and write its number in the space at the left. Write what it is splitting beside that comma's number below the sentence. Next to the other numbers, write the buzzword of the rule for that punctuation. Remember that each set of quotation marks counts as one thing. We will only put a number under the open quote (") mark, not the close quote (") mark.

3 1. After lunch in the afternoon,[1] Grandma would lie down[2] for a while and that was when we had many little,[3] talks.

#1 *2+ intro prep phrases*

#2 *transitive/intransitive verbs*

#3 *splits modifier and its noun*

3 2. "[1]Maddie,[2] you're my favorite grandchild, but I,[3] shouldn't say so," she said one day.

#1 *quotation marks*

#2 *direct address*

#3 *splits subject and verb*

1 3. One day she gave me,[1] her mother's[2] locket and told me it was a secret between her and me[3].

#1 *splits indirect object and direct object*

#2 *possessives*

#3 *which pronoun?*

TRANSITIVE & INTRANSITIVE VERBS: EXERCISE #3

NAME: ______________________________

WHAT TO DO: Circle the correct word in the sentences below.

1. After Grandma gave me the locket, I (sat/set) it carefully on my chest of drawers.
2. I opened my jewelry box and (lay/laid) the locket carefully in it.
3. My mom (raised/rose) me to be careful about family heirlooms like the locket.
4. That night when I (lay/laid) on my bed, I thought about Grandma's stories.
5. When I am an old lady, I'll (sit/set) on the porch and tell them to my grandchildren!

WHAT TO DO: Copy-edit the errors in the following sentences. There are **SEVEN** errors.

Once a year Grandma and her family always, went to the state fair. One year her father took the familys prize hog and he fully expected to get a blue ribbon for that hog! Well the hog was so enormous they almost couldn't get him in the truck. The hog, as a matter of fact wasn't at all interested in climbing up the ramp into the bed of the truck. "Edward go into the kitchen and get that peach cobbler I baked for Mrs. Cramer," said Great-Grandma. Uncle edward grabbed the peach cobbler, climbed into the bed of the truck, and that old hog went racing up the ramp!

WHAT TO DO: In each sentence below there is a comma split. In the spaces below each sentence are the numbers of all the other punctuation in the sentence. Find the comma split and write its number in the space at the left. Write what it is splitting beside that comma's number below the sentence. Next to the other numbers, write the buzzword of the rule for that punctuation. Remember that each set of quotation marks counts as one thing. We will only put a number under the open quote (") mark, not the close quote (") mark.

2 1. The hog's (1) name was Baxter, and Uncle Edward hurled, (2) that pie at him yelling, "Baxter, slow down!" (3)

#1 *possessives*

#2 *splits verb and direct object*

#3 *gear change comma*

3 2. At the sight of that cobbler, (1) it was clear that Baxter (2) had no, (3) idea of slowing down.

#1 *2+ intro prep phrases*

#2 *capitalize*

#3 *splits modifier and its noun*

1 3. Uncle Edward, (1) took one look at Baxter, (2) turned as as white as a sheet, and vaulted over the side of the truck like an Olympic (3) gymnast!

#1 *splits subject and verb*

#2 *items in a series*

#3 *capitalize*

TEST: TRANSITIVE & INTRANSITIVE VERBS

NAME: ______________________________

POINTS EARNED: ________ out of 27 LEVEL: ____________________

WHAT TO DO: Circle the correct word in the sentences below.

__1. After he got into the truck and ate all the cobbler, Baxter (lay/laid) down quietly for the rest of the trip.
1

__2. Great-grandma (sat/set) her prize peach preserves on the seat next to her.
1

__3. Hope (raised/rose) up in her heart when she thought about winning a blue ribbon for those preserves.
1

__4. She and Great-grandpa had (sat/set) their hearts on winning.
1

__5. When the truck went over a bump, Great-grandma picked up her preserves and then carefully (lay/laid) them on her lap for the rest of the trip.
1

WHAT TO DO: Copy-edit the errors in the following sentences. There are **SEVEN** errors.

"We knew we were at the fair when we could hear, the music coming from the carnival" said Grandma. "I was so, excited that I was going to spend the entire day enjoying myself. The sounds, the sight and the smells were just wonderful. Pa and Ma, needless to say, gave us kids a little money to spend at the midway. By noon, however, we had to find Baxters pen to see our enormous beautiful hog as he ~~laid~~ lay in his straw."

__
7

===
12

WHAT TO DO: In each sentence below there is a comma split. In the spaces below each sentence are the numbers of all the other punctuation in the sentence. Find the comma split and write its number in the space at the left. Write what it is splitting beside that comma's number below the sentence. Next to the other numbers, write the buzzword of the rule for that punctuation. Remember that each set of quotation marks counts as one thing. We will only put a number under the open quote (") mark, not the close quote (") mark.

3 (2)

1. Mr. Hiram Hooker was head of the judging committee, and he, looked Baxter over from head to tail.
   (Mr. = 1; committee, = 2; he, = 3)

   (1) #1 *capitalize*

   (1) #2 *compound sentence*

   (1) #3 *splits subject and verb*

3 (2)

2. After a brief conference with the committee, he announced, "Baxter wins, First Prize!"
   (committee, = 1; " = 2; wins, = 3)

   (1) #1 *2+ intro prep phrases*

   (1) #2 *quotation marks*

   (1) #3 *splits verb and direct object*

1 (2)

3. "Pa, Tom, Ed, and I, went to find Ma," said Grandma, "and she was standing there with her preserves, a big grin, and the Blue Ribbon!"
   (I, = 1; Grandma, = 2; preserves, = 3)

   (1) #1 *splits subject and verb*

   (1) #2 *gear change comma*

   (1) #3 *items in a series*

===
15

Score Range		Result
27 - 24	=	Mastery
23 - 22	=	Superiority
21 - 19	=	Competency
18 - 16	=	Probationary
15 and below	=	Repeat